WHO AM I?
WHAT DO I WANT?

Many of us have never really asked—or answered—these crucial questions. Yet every day, week, month and year, we make choices—tens of thousands of them—that greatly influence our chances for failure or *success*. Now Shad Helmstetter, the brilliant behavioral researcher and bestselling author of *What to Say When You Talk to Yourself*, helps us determine the *critical* choices, big and small, that govern us—and shows us how we *make* them. How can we avoid making negative choices? What should we do when we *feel* boxed in, *reacting* to the world instead of *responding* to it—by choice?

———

"WE *DO* LIVE OUT THE LIVES THAT OUR PROGRAMMING CREATES FOR US. AND ANY OF US, WHEN WE CHOOSE, CAN GIVE OURSELVES NEW PROGRAMS! WHAT AN INCREDIBLE OPPORTUNITY THAT FACT GIVES YOU. THE CHOICES YOU MAKE *NEXT* ARE UP TO *YOU*. THAT IS WHAT THIS BOOK IS ALL ABOUT. . . ."

Shad Helmstetter

EACH DAY THAT PASSES,
YOUR CHOICES WILL COME AND GO.

THEY ARE LIKE DIAMONDS
IN A CHEST OF JEWELS,
EACH WAITING TO BE DISCOVERED.

Books by Shad Helmstetter

Choices
Finding the Fountain of Youth Inside Yourself
Predictive Parenting: What to Say When You Talk to
    Your Kids
The Self-Talk Solution
What to Say When You Talk to Yourself
You Can Excel in Times of Change

Published by POCKET BOOKS

CHOICES

SHAD HELMSTETTER

POCKET BOOKS

New York   London   Toronto   Sydney   Tokyo   Singapore

POCKET BOOKS, a division of Simon & Schuster Inc.
1230 Avenue of the Americas, New York, NY 10020

ISBN: 0-671-67419-6

First Pocket Books paperback printing September 1990

10 9 8 7 6 5 4 3

POCKET and colophon are registered trademarks of
Simon & Schuster Inc.

Printed in the U.S.A.

This book is dedicated to my sons, Anthony and Gregory Helmstetter:

To my son Anthony, who taught me the meaning of making good choices. He has been, from childhood to adult, one of the finest individuals I have ever known. He is, in every sense of the word, exceptional. He has contributed more to my life than I could ever express. I would like to be more like him.

And to my son Gregory, who makes "making good choices" a way of life. He, too, is an unending source of inspiration for me and for others.

Together, these two children—now grown young men—have proved to me the unending value of the meaning of "choices"—and what making good choices can mean in the lives of all of us.

CONTENTS

"No one else can ever make your choices for you.

■

Your choices are yours alone.

■

They are as much a part of you as every breath you will take, every moment of your life."

INTRODUCTION: THE STORY OF NACI AND T'NACI

THERE WERE IN ANCIENT TIMES two twins, orphaned from birth.

The two infants, who were twin boys, were left on the steps of the royal palace by their mother, who was wise beyond her years. One of the orphans was named Naci, and the other was named T'naci. The two were identical in every way.

The orphaned twins were beautiful children. It was clear to the palace guards, even when they first found them, that these two infants possessed unusual qualities. When the king and queen—who were without children themselves—first saw the twins, they too knew that the infants were gifted. And so they took them into the palace, and agreed to raise the orphan children as their own.

The only legacy left to each twin was a most unusual deck of twelve cards. And these unusual cards which each of them carried were also identical in every way.

The king and queen were overjoyed with the blessing of receiving the two infants, and they raised them with all of the love and attention that they would have given to their own children.

The new parents decided to wait before revealing to

the twins that they were a blessing that the king and queen had long prayed for. When the time was right, they would tell them. And when Naci and T'naci became old enough, at the age of twenty, the king and queen brought their two young sons to them, and told them of their birth.

It was then that they gave each of their sons the special cards that had been carefully wrapped close to them when they were first found, twenty years before.

"Your first mother must have loved you very much," the queen told them. "When she brought you to us, she also left two identical and most unusual decks of cards. On these cards are written, front and back, the choices you will have to make in the life that is in front of you."

And then she said, in the most loving way, "These simple cards will guide you now more than the king or I could ever guide you through the life that awaits you. Take them, use them, and always remember that we have always loved you and we have always wanted the best for you."

And so Naci and T'naci left the comfort of their home to seek their fortunes.

In the years that followed, Naci learned to read the cards his mother had left with him, but T'naci put them aside, and went his way without seeking their counsel. And while Naci prospered, increased his knowledge, and always seemed to do well, his brother T'naci floundered. From time to time they would meet and talk, but there was a growing difference between them.

"Why is it you do so well when I struggle and fail?" T'naci would ask.

"Perhaps it is because you have not listened to our mother," Naci would reply. "Perhaps it is because you do not use the cards. I have learned to read each of them, each morning of every day, and when I do, things seem to go better for me. Why don't you read our mother's cards for yourself? If you do, perhaps things will go better with you."

But T'naci did not. In time, Naci became well-known, and successful in his own right. But T'naci refused to follow the ideas that his mother's cards inspired, and his fortune fell to failure. While Naci prospered, T'naci fought to succeed, and only failed worse.

Within a few short years, it was time for the two brothers to return home to the palace of their parents. It was time for a new ruler to be named, and one of them was to be the chosen one.

Both of them returned home at the appointed time, and both were met with kind and loving joy from the king and queen. Both of them had always been thought to be special, and they were received with all of the affection that any parent could give.

But there was a difference now. Naci had somehow succeeded in his life where T'naci had not. And T'naci could not understand why.

The day finally came for the king and queen to declare that there would be a new, wise ruler in the land. It was a difficult day for all of them. After all, both sons had been raised in the same way. Both of them had been given the same education. And both of them had been given every possible chance to succeed.

The question that weighed heavily on the minds of the king and the queen and all of the royal advisors was, "Why has one son succeeded while the other son has not?"

It was not until they all gathered together at the Royal Announcement Ball that they were to learn the answer. As you might suspect, in their most caring way, the king and queen announced that Naci was named heir to the throne.

"Why," T'naci asked, "why did my brother gain the throne when in every way we are the same? What did he do that was so different from me?" And it was at the same Royal Announcement Ball that Naci gave the answer.

Naci spoke to the gathered council in a firm, strong voice. He said, "Many years ago my mother, for good reasons, left me on the steps of this palace. And in the basket that held me, she left me a gift. The gift was wrapped in a small cloth, and written on the cloth were the words, 'This is the only gift, beyond my love for you, that I can give you. Take it, and when it is time, use this gift to create the life that I would have wished for you.'

"Wrapped in that cloth was a deck of cards that my mother had written in her own hand. On each card was a challenge, and on the other side of each of those precious cards was a choice. I am here today because of those simple cards, and the choices they presented to me."

And then, in the same clear, strong voice, young Naci read what his mother had written on the cards many long years before.

"On the first card are written the words, CHOOSE YOUR STRENGTH. On the other side of that same card are the words, *I am strong*, and then the words, *I am not strong*.

"On the second card is written the challenge, CHOOSE YOUR HONESTY. On the other side of that card are the words, *I am honest*, and then the words, *I am not honest*.

"The third card says, CHOOSE YOUR BELIEF IN YOURSELF. The other side of the card says, *I believe in myself*, and *I do not believe in myself*.

"The fourth card says, CHOOSE YOUR GOAL AND DIRECTION. On the back of that card it says, *I have chosen my goal and direction and I know what it is*. It also says, *I have not chosen my goal and direction*.

"On the fifth card are written the words, CHOOSE TO ACCEPT OTHERS AS THEY ARE. On the back it says, *I accept others as they are*, and then the words, *I do not accept others as they are*.

"The sixth card says, CHOOSE TO MAKE YOUR DECISIONS FOR YOURSELF. The other side of this most special card says, *I choose to make my decisions for myself*, and it also adds the words, *I do not choose to make my decisions for myself*.

"On the seventh card the words say, CHOOSE TO ALWAYS BE RESPONSIBLE FOR YOUR OWN AC-

TIONS. On the other side of the seventh card is written, *I am responsible for my own actions,* and the words, *I am not responsible for my own actions.*

"On the eighth card is written the challenge, CHOOSE RIGHT FROM WRONG, and it is followed by the words on the second side of the card, *I always do my best to choose right from wrong,* and that is followed by the second phrase, *I do not choose to choose right from wrong.*

"The ninth card says, CHOOSE TO WORK FOR WHAT YOU BELIEVE IN, and on the other side of this card are the words, *I always choose to work for what I believe in,* and then the words, *I do not make the choice to work for what I believe in.*

"The tenth card reads, CHOOSE TO LEARN FROM YOUR MISTAKES, and on the back of the card are the phrases, *I choose to learn from my mistakes,* and *I choose not to learn from my mistakes.*

"On the eleventh card are the words, CHOOSE TO LOVE AND BE LOVED, and on the back of the card it says, *I choose to love and be loved,* followed by a second choice, *I choose not to love and be loved.*

"The twelfth card is perhaps the most important of these simple cards. It says, CHOOSE TO CHOOSE IN EVERY DETAIL OF YOUR LIFE. The other side of this card says, *I choose to choose,* and that is followed by the words, *I do not choose to choose.*"

And then young Naci said, "These are the words which my mother left me. These are the words which I have chosen to live by. These twelve simple choices have served me well. With them, as your servant, I hope to serve you well."

*"You may think that in life,
a lot of things happen to you
along the way.*

■

*The truth is, in life, you
happen to a lot of things
along the way."*

1

THE TRUTH
ABOUT CHOICES

THIS IS A BOOK about choices—whether we have them or not, how to make them, which choices are really important and which only seem to be. And, most important, why some of us can learn to make good choices but never seem to be able to stick to them.

Do We Have Free Will?

There have been many arguments both for and against the concept of free will. Philosophers and theologians throughout history have discussed this question. They are still talking about it. Are we, as individuals, able to choose for ourselves?

Are we able to set our own path, chart our own course and follow it? Or is there something outside us—or within us—that ultimately is at the helm? Do we steer our own course, or does some autopilot step in and take over for us?

If you are traveling down the road in an automobile, is it you who is doing the driving, or is it someone else? Who or what is turning the steering wheel, setting the speed, and stopping or starting the car in the first place?

Who, or what, is really in control of you? Who is in

charge—not only of the big decisions you make in life, but of each small step along the way, what you do with every breath you take?

That's an important question, because unless you decide that you do have a choice—at least *some* "free will"—it is unlikely that you would exercise any free will that you had in the first place.

In this book, we're not going to debate the issue. And we're not going to debate the notion of whether or not we are driven by a spiritual predestination. We are not questioning whether or not there is a guiding force that infuses the universe with energy and determines the destiny of humankind. We're not talking here about anything so grand.

The Practical Choices of Everyday Life

This book deals instead with the most practical choices of our daily lives. And it shows how those choices determine our direction in almost anything we do. Together, those choices create our success and failures in life.

What makes your day a "bad day" or a "good day"? Whom do you talk to? What do you say? If you drive a car, how fast or slow do you generally drive, and why? Do you get upset easily, or do you usually remain calm and collected?

Do you think things through, work at them and see them through to their conclusion, or do you drop something before it's finished and move on to something else? Do you get along well with others in your family? How do you spend your spare time?

What do you do, and why? If you are an adult and have or will have a family, how many children do you have, or how many will you have, and why will you have that number? What makes you angry, or what makes you excited and happy? Will you get the promotion or won't you? Will you get a "B+" on the test, or will you get a "C"?

Each of these questions, and thousands more like them, involves choices. Each of us has the right as an individual to make the choices that we want to make for ourselves, and to become the master of our own destiny—the one and only true captain of our own ship.

Can we accomplish this great feat simply by deciding to *choose*—by making the decision to make choices? As we will see, we *do* have a free will; there is nothing that can drive us against our own wishes, and there is a way we *can* learn to make all those choices, big and small, for ourselves.

Each of us does have free agency; we can choose for ourselves anything we'd like to choose, and as long as it doesn't break laws or conflict with the social order, we can achieve a life of self-fulfillment by living out the choices we make for ourselves.

It is a way of telling the world, "You go ahead and stumble along, world—you lead other people astray if you like, but from here on out, I'm taking control of my own future. I'm putting my *self* in charge of my own life. I'll sit in the driver's seat, thank you, and steer for myself!"

What Stops It from Working?

We have learned that making the decision to choose for ourselves is one thing, but doing it and continuing to do it, choice by choice, day after day, month after month, year after year, is quite another thing.

There are others who tell us that we may not actually have any *true* choices at all. There are scientists and researchers who, in spite of what they would like to believe, have become convinced by their research that we are all ultimately the product of our genes and programming.

They tell us that even though we *think* we are making choices for ourselves, we are actually doing nothing more than reacting to the world around us and responding in a chemically and electrically programmed way. They claim that we are so much the result of our programming and our genetic chemical structures that even our choices— our decisions—are predetermined by our programs.

And there are others who are equally convinced that our minds are battlefields on which the saga of good versus evil is played out with Right and Wrong each trying to convince us to go its way, with the outcome of our choices leading us to spiritual success or failure.

In that battle, we are told not only that our choices determine our successes and failures, but also that these choices determine whether we save or lose our souls.

There are others who tell us that each of us creates our own reality, that what we create in our minds will become manifest in our lives. They tell us that we are at least in part—or perhaps entirely—responsible for not only the role that we play in life, but even for what happens to us in the world.

This popular philosophy suggests that although we are a holistic part of the "cosmic whole," we are in fact at the centers of our own individual universes, and we create those universes—for what they are—by our own choices.

And so we have philosophies, religions, political ideologies and parental values all presented to us as ways to live more successfully—and many of them are in complete conflict and disagreement with one another.

Wars have been fought over less.

But what about the practical, day-to-day "I'm trying my best to do my best" approach to choices? When it comes right down to it, few of the world's great philosophies seem all that important when it comes to getting the kids off to school on time or deciding which program to watch on television.

So let's find out what our choices really are, how much control each of us really has in making those choices work for us, what stops us or holds us back, and what we can do about it.

An amazing thing happens when people learn to focus on their choices in a new, *self-directed* way. Something "clicks" inside and we suddenly realize that finding the *courage to change* is no more difficult than learning to make one small choice at a time.

By the end of this book, you may find that you have more control over your life *each and every day* than you might have imagined. People who learn more about choices, and *how* to make more choices for themselves, learn that not only do they have *hope*, but they literally are able to give themselves the mechanism and the opportunity to change.

"Choosing to live your life
by your own choice

∎

Is the greatest freedom you
will ever have."

2

WHO ARE YOU AND WHAT DO YOU WANT?

A NUMBER OF YEARS AGO, before I began writing about Self-Management and personal potential, I began conducting a special kind of personal training session for a few individuals.

In these weekend-long sessions I had the opportunity to take one or two individuals at a time through an in-depth review of their lives up to that moment. The object was to bring them up-to-date and face to face with who they really were, and what they *really* wanted out of life.

My reason for holding these sessions was that it seemed to me that all too many individuals I met often spoke about how frustrated they were with where they were in life; they did not feel that they were living up to the potential they wanted to reach.

Many of these individuals were "successful"—that is, they had most of the "indicators" of success. They held responsible jobs, they had uplifting personal and spiritual lives, they were raising families or had already raised them, and they had most of the comforts of life that "success" usually brings.

But they were not fulfilled. They felt, inside, that there was more to the potential of life than they were

19

living. And they didn't know how to go about doing anything about it.

Each of the individuals who spent a solid weekend in those sessions looking inward—and outward—told me later that he or she had found part of the answer, and with each individual, his or her life changed in some noticeable ways.

In one of those early programs, one of my attendees was a woman named Kathy. She was a woman who appeared to have all of the attributes for success—looks, talent, skills, and attitude. But Kathy believed that she would always be overweight, and would never have the talent or skill to get ahead in her career as a sales representative for a large electronics firm.

Following the two days of the simple "self-retraining" that she experienced, Kathy lost sixteen unwanted pounds, kept them off, and got to work on some solid career-growth steps that changed her position and her long-term career.

Another individual, Kurt, who had flown to my city from his home 2,000 miles away, attended one of the early programs. Kurt was a man who appeared to have everything. He had a good job as an executive with an aircraft company, a fine family, and what appeared to be nothing but success in front of him.

But Kurt was unhappy with himself. He felt he wasn't in the job he really wanted to be in, and even though his family looked great from the outside, he told me that things were not going well at home either.

A few months after Kurt had attended the program, he wrote to tell me that he had made some astounding changes in his life. He had gone to his company's managers and requested (and received) a change in jobs—to a job he was completely happy in. Kurt had also made some changes at home. He spent more time working on making his family life work, and it was working *better* than he had hoped.

And there were others—people with the same kinds of very real frustrations, making small but exceptionally important changes in their lives. For me, watching people change their futures by reevaluating *who they really were and what they really wanted out of life,* opened doors in personal growth that never closed.

What I first learned from those early, small discoveries was that many of us live out our lives without ever stopping long enough to look back to where we came from, figure out who we are now—*today*—and set new sights on the life that waits in front of us.

I had called that early "personal assessment" program "WHO ARE YOU AND WHAT DO YOU WANT?" I thought at the time that I should write a book on the subject. In that book I planned to outline the simple steps that anyone could go through to reevaluate the past, get a new picture of his or her *"self"* today, and make better choices for the future. I did not know then that it would be almost twenty years before my book on that subject would be written.

At the time I had never heard of something called "Self-Talk," or "Self-Management," or "Self-Programming." Those were discoveries in personal growth that were yet to come.

Twenty years ago even the word "programming" had a different connotation. We didn't have personal computers yet, and we knew very little about how the human brain is, in some ways, much like a personal computer. Most of us did not know then that the brain does get "programmed" from everything we hear from the world around us, and from our own "Self-Talk"—*everything* we say when we talk to ourselves.

Knowing what we have now learned about how the human brain—and mind—actually works, I am surprised that those few individuals who first attended weekend sessions on "WHO ARE YOU AND WHAT DO YOU WANT?" got anything at all from their two-day "self" evaluations. But as I was to learn, we had, without knowing it, discovered a *part* of the answer: *they had explored, for the first time, the true CHOICES that were in front of them.*

But they did have only a *part* of the answer. Making "*choices,*" it appeared, was important. But the rest of the answer lay in how to make the *right* choices in the first place—and then in how to make those choices *work!*

Imagine spending twelve or sixteen hours a day for two full days outlining a *complete picture* of who you *thought* you were and what you have wanted out of life up to now, and ending up with a completely new, up-to-date picture of who you really are today. And then, imagine being handed that exciting new picture of yourself—and realizing, maybe for the first time, what you *could* do—starting tomorrow.

We're Finally Making Progress

Now, years later, we have learned more about ourselves. Neuroscientists, mind/brain scientists, and behavioral researchers have gained incredible new ground in unlocking the secrets of the human brain. And what they have learned has taught *us* vital new information about making choices, and how making the right choices—*in the right way*—can affect our lives and our futures in almost unimaginable ways.

After nearly twenty years, we are again ready to ask the questions, "Who are you?" and "What do you want?" And this time, when you answer the questions, you will have some help in making the right choices, and in making your choices work.

That's important. Unless you understand *what makes some of your choices work—while other choices do not,* you may make decisions that are important to you. However, you may never have the advantage of knowing how to give yourself the Self-Programming that will put your important choices into *action*—and keep them working for you *permanently*.

Louis, an elderly friend of mine, told me that he had read and practiced many of the ideas he had learned from books that dealt with "taking control of your life."

But Louis was constantly stopped or frustrated by

how *difficult* some of those same choices were to maintain. "I really believe," Louis told me, "that the authors who write the books on making decisions and making choices for yourself are on the right track. But accepting what they tell you is one thing. *Doing* it is another."

Jeanne, a mother of four, told me, "My life really started to get better when I decided to make choices for myself about what I really wanted and what I wanted for my family. But then it got difficult. Staying with the decisions I've made has been one of the hardest things I have ever done—and I'm not sure I'm winning the battle."

The president of a manufacturing firm told me that when he decided on a three-year plan for managing his company to reach his goal, he thought that it was one of the best decisions he had ever made. And then he added, "It was also one of the toughest decisions I have ever had to face, day after day. How do you keep it working when sometimes you are your own worst enemy?"

Each of these people had the best of intentions. Each of them had decided to "make choices." Each of them had recognized that unless we make conscious choices about ourselves and our futures, we leave most of what happens to us up to chance.

But all of them, like so many others, had also come to learn that following through with even the *best* of choices, and making them work, often proved to be an impossible task—*even when the choice they made was the RIGHT choice in the first place*.

Now, years later, I have had the opportunity to conduct seminars based on the concept of "Who Are You And What Do You Want?." I have had the chance to talk to many of the participants of those seminars, and I have watched, sometimes firsthand, the results in their lives.

There is not space in this book to ask you all of the questions that those seminar attendees are asked in person. But you can get an idea.

Who you are *now*, and what you really want out of

life *today*, is always the result of the programming—the influences—that have come from your past. It works like this:

- Who you have been up until now is the result of the programs you have received up until now.
- What you have wanted from yourself and from life up until now has been the result of those same programs.
- Who you *are*, beginning today, is the result of the *new* choices you start to make today.
- What you really want out of life, *now*, is also up to the choices that you decide to make now.

Most of us know that making the decision to make choices about what we do in our lives is part and parcel of making things work for us. And most of us who have worked at making choices also know that the problem is *us! We* are the roadblock that gets in the way of making our choices work.

There is a way to make good choices. It is a way that almost anyone can learn.

Who Are You and What Do You Want?— A Personal Review

To find out how to make choices that work, and to find out how to make those choices work, day after day, let's go back to those two, all-important, basic questions: "Who are you?" and "What do you want?"

To ask those questions in the right way, you have to ask yourself, "Who am I *really?*" and "What do I *really* want?" To help you find out who you really are and what you really want, there are a few questions you may want to ask yourself.

If you would like to get the most out of the questions that I ask you in the following self-quiz, I would suggest that you take the time to think about each of your answers and write them out. There is nothing like having to write well-thought-out answers to help you become abundantly aware how much of your life up until now has created the programming that you carry with you today and the beliefs that you have about yourself now.

But if you do nothing more than read the questions to yourself and then answer each question for yourself, even without writing your answers down, you will begin to get the picture.

The questions in this self-quiz have no right or wrong answers. They are not some form of "self-therapy." These are questions that will help you recognize where you have been up to now, what helped form and shape the "you" that you are today, and where you might like to take that "you" in the future.

The following self-quiz is easy to take. It should be fun, and it will probably be very revealing. Try to do it in writing as that tends to help organize your thoughts. But if you don't have the time just answer the questions to yourself. The *answers* you get could be very important to you.

As you answer the following questions, be *extremely* honest in your answers. Imagine that you are talking to your most trusted friend in the world. You are. You're talking to yourself.

WHO ARE YOU AND WHAT DO YOU WANT?

PART I
WHO *WERE* YOU? (WHO HAVE YOU BEEN UP TO NOW?)

1. When were you born?

2. Describe your childhood.

3. Who and what influenced you the most—and how and why?

4. How did you see yourself when you were growing up? (Smart or not so smart, capable, happy, average, etc.)

5. How did you typically imagine you would be when you grew up?

6. If you could change something about your childhood, what would you change?

PART II
WHAT *DID* YOU WANT? (WHAT DID YOU THINK YOU WANTED UP TO NOW?)

1. Did you have goals about your future?

2. What did you want to do for a living?

3. Describe the family life you wanted to have.

4. What did you want your financial status to be?

5. Where did you want to live, and what kind of home did you want to live in?

6. How did you want to spend your personal or spare time?

7. How much education did you want to have?

8. When you were young, what did you "want to be when you grew up?"

PART III
WHO ARE YOU *NOW?* (WHO DO YOU REALLY WANT TO BE NOW?)

1. Describe the type of person you would most like to be now.

2. Do other people see you as the person you would most like to be now?

3. If you could change or improve three things about yourself now, what would they be?

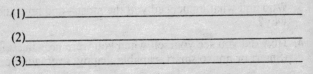

(1)_____

(2)_____

(3)_____

4. What (if anything) is standing in your way at the present time, and keeping you from being the person you would most like to be?

(1)_____

(2)_____

(3)_____

5. Are you now the person you really wanted to be?

PART IV

WHAT DO YOU *REALLY* WANT? **(If you could now *choose*—realistically—to have what you really want to have in your life, what would you choose?)**

1. What do you really want to be doing for a living?

2. Where do you really want to live?

3. How much income do you really want to earn?

4. What do you really want your family life to be like?

5. How do you really want to spend your spare time—what do you *really* want to be doing when you're not working or meeting other obligations?

6. Describe the future you would really like to have (realistically), if you could create it or direct it from here on out.

7. Is there anything else that you really want, in any area of your life, that you do not now have and could realistically attain?

_____

_____

What did you find out? Are you the person you have accepted yourself to be? Or are you, in any way, *different* from that person? Are there some things you would like to do differently, beginning today or tomorrow, if you *could*?

Our Answers Can Lead Us to Choices That Help

One woman who attended a recent seminar program on this subject told me later that after sitting through three days of answering questions about her past, she first discovered the patterns in her upbringing that created patterns that she was living out today as an adult.

"Not only did I learn where my programming came from," she said, "but I also learned where I got a lot of the roadblocks that I have been putting in front of myself. One thing I learned is why I have always believed that it would never be right for me to have enough money," she said. "I actually thought that it was okay for other people to have nice things. I had always believed that having money was either wrong or it was for someone else to have—never me!

"And look at me," she said. "Look at what I've been doing to myself! Almost every choice I've made about money, even after I became an adult, has helped to make it impossible for me to have any."

One man who had gone through the same question and answer process in another seminar told me, "I was sent away from my home when I was twelve years old. After that I lived with a lot of different people and I lived in a lot of different places," he said.

"I can't believe it! For the last forty years I've been trying to prove to myself and to everyone I met that I was worthy of belonging here in the first place."

Another seminar attendee, a close friend of mine, told me later, "Having to answer those questions taught me a whole lot about myself. I certainly learned why I have been making my choices the way I have been. All these years I've been trying to live up to my dad's expectations. My dad was a great guy, but I have my own life to live." And then he added, "I also learned that I've always wanted to play a musical instrument. I'm going to do that."

I myself cannot remember a single day—since the time in high school when one of my counselors sat down and talked to me—that I was ever encouraged by anyone to decide for myself who I really wanted to be and what I really wanted out of life.

It can be a rude awakening to come to the realization that all too many of the choices we have been making in our lives have been choices that did nothing more than help us to get by, cause us to live up to the expectations of others, hold us back, or stop us from living out most of the real potential that we were born with. It is exciting to recognize that it is the choices we make now and in the future that can help us change that.

We Live Out the Lives That Our Programming Creates

What brought you to where you are *now* is your *programming*. You are, for the most part, the sum total of your genetic structure (that you were born with) and the programming that you received from others—and from yourself—since you were born.

You can—if you choose—from here on out, give *yourself* the programs that create for you, in yourself, the person you would most like to be.

That means that you can—if you choose—start right now to make *new* choices for yourself. It means that you can, with your own *Self*-Programming, *make the choices that are best for you, and give your "self" the internal self-directing programs that will make your choices work!*

In the books *WHAT TO SAY WHEN YOU TALK TO YOURSELF* and *THE SELF-TALK SOLUTION* I told the story, in everyday terms, of what we have learned about the human brain. I also discussed how to make our minds work better for us, in a very practical way, and I compared the brain to a computer-like organ that collects information, stores it, and acts on the information it receives—whether the information we feed to it is true or not.

Self-Talk is a method that anyone can use to consciously create strong new self-directed programs safely and naturally—in his or her subconscious mind. Self-Talk overrides earlier negative mental programs and replaces them with programs that create better attitudes, better actions and better results. It works the same way the brain was programmed in the first place—but this time the individual is in charge of the "input" or what gets "programmed in."

The purpose of those two books was to show how the brain gets programmed, and what specific "Self-Talk" we can use to create new, better programs in the brain.

Whatever we say to ourselves—whatever Self-Talk we feed to our subconscious mind—the brain programs that information electrically and chemically. That information is then *imprinted—recorded*—in the brain, electrically and chemically.

What the brain is told, *it accepts*, whether what we tell it is true or false, bad or good, positive or negative. *And it is the job of the subconscious mind to ACT OUT the picture of ourselves that we give it.*

The result is that "who we think we are" and "what we think we want" is always the result of the programming that we received from the world around us or from ourselves.

Knowing this, we can now look at ourselves—and our *future*—in a whole new light.

We *do* live out the lives that our programming creates for us. And *ANY OF US, WHEN WE CHOOSE, CAN GIVE OURSELVES NEW PROGRAMS!* What an incredible opportunity that fact gives you. The choices you make *next* are up to *you*. That is what this book is all about.

We have often heard the saying that tells us that "today is the first day of the rest of your life." But that saying may be true only if you are able to actually *do* something about the rest of your life.

But as we shall see, with what we've learned, now there *is* something you can do about it.

*"It is only when you exercise
your right to <u>choose</u>*

■

*That you can also exercise
your right to <u>change</u>."*

THE DILEMMA
OF FREE WILL

THE MORE I LEARNED about the programming processes of the human brain, the more I began to ask myself a very important question: What about free will? Do we really have it?

Researchers learned that the human brain operates very much like a powerful computer and the brain responds to the programs it receives. Some of the brain's programs are genetic—that is, we were born with them. The rest of the brain's programs are received and programmed into the brain beginning at the time of birth and continuing throughout our lives. The researchers also learned that we live our lives based on the many programs that we carry with us in the brain.

The brain is designed to keep us alive; but even more than that, the brain is designed to accept information (through our five senses and our own thoughts), store that information as chemically and electrically imprinted programs in the brain, and cause us to literally live out our lives by acting on the programs which are strongest.

Since that is scientific fact, what does that do to our notion of free will?

The Results of Losing Free Will

Imagine a 16-year-old boy named Eddy, who lives in a ghetto in the worst part of the city, breaking into an appliance store window at 2 o'clock in the morning, grabbing a television from the window display and running with it down the street toward the alley. A patrol car is parked in the alley and the boy is caught. He is tried for his crime, found guilty, and sentenced to a juvenile jail.

But if that young man is the product of his conditioning—the negative mental programs he grew up on in the place where he lived—it is obvious that most of the programs he received were the ones that would teach him to do exactly what he did. If he had different programs chemically and electrically imprinted in the computer control center of his brain, it is entirely possible that he would have made different choices—many different and more positive choices throughout his life.

But in spite of what *caused* the young boy to commit the crime in the first place, he actually went to jail because of his *programs!* Did he have free will or did he not? Let us say that the young boy had gone to school and was reasonably well aware of right and wrong. He had learned what society expected of him; he knew that it was wrong to break the law, and that he would have to pay for the consequences of his actions.

But in spite of the fact that he clearly knew right from wrong, and would seem to have had the free will to choose—considering the negative programming of his past that put him there in the first place—*did he really have free will?*

Here's another example. Preston's parents had always wanted him to be a doctor. Preston himself was more interested in astronomy and, even as a young boy, dreamed of becoming an astronomer. But Preston's parents prevailed, and eventually they convinced him that he should follow the career of their choosing.

After all, they were paying his way through school,

and in spite of the fact that he had grave misgivings about living up to his fullest potential as a doctor, Preston chose to accept his parents' guidance. He eventually became the doctor that his parents had so long wanted him to be.

Later, at the end of his second marriage, and teetering on the edge of almost absolute career frustration, Preston was so upset with himself for making the wrong decision that he felt he had failed his parents, and certainly himself.

But didn't Preston have free will when he made the choice to enter medical school? By most standards he was certainly an adult; he was clear-headed, intelligent, and able to make decisions for himself. If Preston had free will, then why did he make the wrong choice?

Those two examples touch on choices that create life-changing events. But what about the smaller choices in life? If we have free will, then we should be able to make the *right* choices in any decision we make—big *or* small.

Tracy, as an example, is a middle-management supervisor in an electronics company. For years, Tracy has wanted to move into upper management. She has gone back to school to acquire the additional management background and skills necessary for the upper management position she wants to hold. She has prepared herself to move into the job.

But on each occasion during the last year when a position opened up that Tracy was clearly qualified for, she held back until it was too late and someone else filled the position.

Tracy knew she could and would succeed if she was ever put into the management position that she sought. She badly wanted to do what she knew was the right thing—apply for the position. But by waiting too long, in each case she made the choice not to apply. If Tracy had the free will to make the right choice, then why, in each case, did she make the choice that she knew was wrong?

Did she have free will? And if she did, why did she

not exercise her free will so that it would clearly work *for* her instead of against her?

Or how about Carolyn? Carolyn sells cosmetics for a national firm, and she loves her work. But Carolyn has a problem that constantly holds her back—her weight. In the last five years alone, Carolyn has gone on diets a dozen times. Each time she has managed to reach her goal of 127 slim, trim, attractive pounds—only to gain back the pounds she worked so hard to lose.

It's obvious that no one is force-feeding Carolyn. She's doing it herself. It must be her choice. And yet Carolyn will tell you—and she means it—she genuinely wants to take the weight off and keep it off. It's important to her job, and it's important to her self-esteem.

If Carolyn has free will—if no one is forcing her to weigh one pound more than she should—then why does she make the wrong choice when she sits down to eat?

Can We Really Use the Free Will That We Have?

Even school children who have reached the age of reason seem to know the difference between right and wrong, good and bad, and what works and what doesn't. And it also seems that even when they should be able to exercise free will, they—just as we did when we were their age—make choice after choice that is wrong, even when they clearly know better.

We all suffer from the same dilemma. Think of some of the things that you have done against your better judgment—when you knew better. Why do we do it?

Why do we argue when we shouldn't, show up late for work morning after morning, eat or drink too much or the wrong thing, smoke, fail to exercise, drive too fast, put things off even when we know they have to be done, spend too much, marry the wrong mate, knowingly hurt someone else when we could avoid it, and put up with a bad job instead of making a change? Often we ignore responsibilities, fail to spend enough time with our kids, tell lies, get out of school and never go back, let the car run out of gas, let someone bother us daily at work, let ourselves get depressed when we don't have to, not study for tests, or a thousand or so other things that we do or do not do even when *we know better*.

If we have free will, why aren't we using it?! After years of pondering this important question—a question that even philosophers have argued about through the ages—the answer finally became unquestionably clear to me: The free will we are given is stopped by the programs we receive.

The Old Programs That Stop Us

What we suspected is true. Everyone *does* have free will. Most of us *do* know right from wrong. But it is our past *programming*, both from others and from our own harmful Self-Talk, that stops us from exercising our free will.

The teenage boy who steals the television set knows that he is wrong—at least he is certainly aware that it's against the law. But the poor programming of his upbringing put him on a downhill path of bad choices, and all but destroyed any chance he might have had of exercising the free will that he was originally given.

A young man who wants to be an astronomer gives in to the powerful programming of parents and he loses the right to the free will that would have helped him make the correct choice for his career and his life.

A woman lets past mental programs of self-doubt and lack of confidence in her ability, stop her from exercising her free will and making a choice in her career growth she so badly wants to make. A woman who is angry with herself for being unable to lose weight and keep it off allows her past programs of an overweight self-identity to lock her free will in the refrigerator every time she sits down to eat.

Each of them, and all of us, have free will. But it is our old programs—inaccurate, harmful pictures of ourselves as incapable—that sentence us to a lifetime of not quite living up to the potential that the exercise of our free will would have given us.

Our recent understanding of the human brain and how it gets chemically and electrically programmed from birth, for the most part, lays to rest the age-old philosophical question of free will. We now know that we have it, if our own programs don't get in the way.

If you want to make better choices in your life and *really* exercise the free will that you were meant to have, it's a good idea to understand and learn to do something about the programs that could be stopping you.

*"It is your programming
that has created your choices
in the past.*

■

*It is the choices you make
today that are creating
the programs of
your future."*

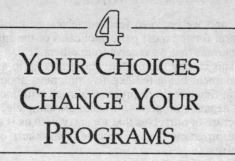

4

YOUR CHOICES
CHANGE YOUR
PROGRAMS

ALL OF US ARE PROGRAMMED from birth with an incredible number of chemically and electrically imprinted programs in the brain that control us and affect us, drive us and direct our behavior every single moment of our lives.

Our programs influence or direct what we think, how we feel, and what we do, day in and day out, in every area of our lives, big and small. The programs that we receive, first from others and then from our own internal Self-Talk, a form of self-programming, are like tens of thousands of major and minor directions to ourselves that are recorded in the brain—much like the programs that we type into the personal computers that we use at home and at work.

Those programs tell us who we are, what we believe, what our attitudes are, and how we feel about anything and everything. At first, those programs come to us by what we are told by others.

We are programmed by our parents, our brothers and sisters, our friends, our teachers at school, and our associates at work. Even while we are very young, those same programs that we get from others begin to form the basis of our own Self-Talk. Then that Self-Talk takes over, and we begin to feed ourselves mental programs that are, for the most part, duplicates of the same kinds of programs that we receive from others.

This is why the person who grows up in a negative environment being fed negative programs about himself will, in time, begin to program himself with more of the same negative programs. In time, the complete, composite picture of ourselves that we carry with us is the result of the programs that we receive from others or give to ourselves.

That is how self-esteem, as an example, is created in each of us. We learn to believe who we are, how we should look, how we act, what we reach for in life or do not reach for, and what we achieve or do not achieve. Those programs, together with the genetic programs that we were born with, combine to make us who we are. Everything you believe about yourself today is the result of those programs.

In its simplest form, this is why one person succeeds in life when another person does not. Those programs create the difference in why we are able to earn the income we want, obtain the education we need, get the job done, keep ourselves mentally and physically fit, get along well with others and have successful relationships, keep stress in check, enjoy our work, take the time to do the things we truly want to do, express ourselves in a positive way, stay reasonably happy most of the time, live with truth and personal integrity, take responsibility for ourselves, and above all, make choices that work for us instead of against us.

It is that same programming which, if it is the wrong kind, influences us in the wrong way and directs us to do the wrong things.

If you give a computer the wrong programs it will do the wrong things. If we have programs that are negative or programs that work against us, those programs *must* give us false or erroneous directions. We live our lives based on the programming we carry with us. That's how the brain works.

What Can You Do About It?

The question then is, what can you do about it? Let's say that *you* were programmed, while you were young and growing up, with the same kinds of programming that most of us received. Some of the programs you received were undoubtedly good—they work for you and they give you the ability to make at least some choices that are the right choices. But most of us also received all too many programs that caused us problems.

In my earlier books, I discussed how basic programming works and what any of us, if we choose, can do to change the programming we received; how to override earlier programs with the right kind of Self-Talk, and how to replace the programs we do not want with more positive programs that help us direct our lives in a more fulfilling way each and every day.

If you are not presently using the new kind of Self-Talk to change or get rid of some of the old programs, I strongly recommend that you learn more about Self-Talk and find out what it can do for you. Many thousands of individuals are now using Self-Talk to change old habits, set new goals, lose weight, earn more income, have more success in personal relationships, become better parents, do better on the job, overcome depression, become more physically fit, build self-esteem, overcome problems and personal limitations, get rid of false pictures of themselves, learn to succeed, and to learn to live—day in and day out—lives that are happier and more fulfilled.

An Important New Way to Change the Old Programs

In addition to learning about Self-Talk, learning how to practice Self-Talk, and/or listening to the strong, precisely worded self-directions on Self-Talk cassettes, what can you do *right now* to give yourself more positive, more productive new programs that will override the old?

Over the years, as I observed people from all walks

of life who were using Self-Talk to put themselves in gear and start moving in the right direction, I began to notice that those individuals who were practicing Self-Talk on a daily basis were, without even knowing about it, giving themselves an additional reprogramming tool. Because of the Self-Talk, *they were making different choices*.

The choices those Self-Talkers were making were, time after time, more of the choices that they had really wanted to make all along. Since it was their old programming that had gotten in the way of making good choices in the first place, it only makes sense that when they gave themselves new programming, they were able to make better choices. And more important, they were arming themselves with the mental self-directives that would *support* the new choices and make them work. But it was the new choices themselves that time after time proved to make the final difference in how well their lives were working for them.

That one simple act of human behavior by itself—the act of making choices—sets in motion a pattern of belief, a determined sense of self-will that tells the brain: "This is how I choose to be. This is how I want to become."

Choices Create Programs in the Brain

That one fact gives each of us the incredible opportunity to begin to change our old, negative programs right now, today—and to replace those old programs that held us back with a whole new set of programs that work *for* us!

The act of making good choices—and along with making those choices, giving yourself the absolute determination to see them through—sets up a chain reaction of results in the mind that begins to slowly but surely replace or override bad programming.

We have learned that programming creates choices.

What we have learned since then is that *choices create programming*. That's exciting!

This means that if you make the decision to make good choices, and demand of yourself that you will stick by those choices moment by moment, day by day, those simple but all-important choices will in turn create new programming. This new programming is the kind that gives you the edge, puts you on top, puts you back in control, and gives you the chance to take charge of your life.

Old, negative programming sounds like this:

- "I just can't do it."
- "I just know it won't work."
- "I'm not cut out for that."
- "I'm not creative enough."
- "I never have enough money."
- "I can't get along with my boss."
- "I never seem to have the time I need to get everything done."
- "She's better than I am."
- "I lose weight and then I gain it right back again."
- "Some people have all the luck."
- "I never get anyplace on time."
- "I'll never be a straight-A student."
- "I just can't seem to get organized."
- "I can't make my marriage work."
- "I get nervous just thinking about speaking in front of a group."
- "I just know it's going to be another one of *those* days."

From the important to the mundane, our Self-Talk goes on and on—leading us, pulling us, and directing us in so many wrong directions.

The truth is, every one of those negative, work-against-us Self-Talk phrases is a *choice*.

An Exciting Opportunity
to Create New Programs

When we allow those almost unconscious, unnoticed Self-Talk choices to have free reign in our minds, we are not aware that those choices are setting us up. It is those choices that are telling us: "**This** is how you are. **This** is the best you can hope for. **This** is what you can expect from yourself. **This** is how it's going to be."

Every time you state another negative choice to yourself, you give yourself another program. The new negative program that you just gave to yourself joins hands with the other programs that you already carry with you in your mind and, together, they reaffirm your belief in what you cannot do or what will not work for you.

It makes no difference whether what others told you, and what you eventually learned to tell yourself, was true or not.

That, too, is how the brain works. The facet of the brain that we call the subconscious mind simply accepts the programs that you give it, imprints those programs (whether beneficial or detrimental) as *facts*—as *truths*—about who you are, and then goes to work to act them out.

And therein lies an exciting opportunity. The same brain—the one that works so hard to accept your negative Self-Talk choices, program them in, imprint them, and get you to act them out as though they are *true*—will also accept, program, and act on other kinds of choices, the "positive" or *better* choices.

The result of this almost unnoticed but powerful aspect of the workings of the human brain can be made to work for us instead of against us.

The choices you make today will create programs in your mind. Those programs will begin to affect you and direct you, just as the brain has accepted and implemented the choices—the programs—that we have given it in the past.

Let's say that you decide, right now, to make a choice to change something in your life. Let's make it something simple. Let's say that you decide to choose to get along better with someone you know. You could state that choice like this: "I really get along well with _____ ." (You fill in the name.)

Let's say in the past you liked this person. It could be your spouse, a son or daughter, a parent, your boss at work, or a friend. Or, it may even be true that the person in question is not someone with whom you have gotten along well in the past. It makes no difference. The new choice—the new self-direction—the new *program* to your subconscious mind is: "I have chosen to get along well with this person."

Let's also assume that when you make this choice, it is a strong, solid, clear, determined choice to take action and make the relationship work.

Look at what powerful chemistry you put into play in the brain! First, you make the choice. Next, you state your choice in a clear and simple statement of your objective. Now you give that message clearly and consciously to your own computer control center—your brain, and your subconscious mind.

The brain picks up the message and accepts it as a new directive. (In the subconscious mind, that's what it does.) Now let's say, because you're determined, that you give that same message to your brain and your subconscious mind repeatedly, with belief and determination.

Based on what we now know about the programming processes of the human brain, what must your brain do with the new directive that you are now giving it? Because of the way the subconscious mind operates, it *must act* on the new directives you are giving it.

One of the rules that governs the subconscious mind is that *the strongest program always wins*. The brain follows the strongest directions which we give it. We direct and the brain accepts. And what the brain accepts, it *must* act on. If you give yourself the same strong, clear self-direction repeatedly, the brain will tirelessly go to work to put your new direction into practice.

At first you'll notice yourself talking in a different way to the individual you want to get along with. Your behavior will change in some ways that are subtle and some ways that are obvious. It will change.

If your behavior could possibly have anything to do with the outcome of that relationship, you can be sure that the relationship will change. If the probability or the possibility of success in the relationship is there in the first place, then your one simple choice—your directive to your own subconscious mind—will go to work to begin making the change you hoped to achieve.

Choose any example you'd like and give it the same test. If the chance for success is there in the first place, your change in self-direction will set the result in motion.

Try It for Yourself

Try this tomorrow: Find something you would like to change, make a choice to change it, and put your choice in simple words. Write your choice down on a 3 × 5 index card. Carry it with you and read it at every opportunity throughout the day, every day for the next three weeks.

You won't achieve any lifelong goals overnight, perhaps, but you will notice a change. You may notice a change in what happens around you—in whatever it is that you are trying to affect and improve. But you should especially notice the change that happens in yourself; *that's* the change you are looking for.

If you want to change your programs, change your choices. State them, write them down if you like, get a clear picture in your own mind of the results you want to achieve, and turn your *choice* into a *program*.

Don't stop yourself because the method sounds too simple. As complex as the internal neurological programming and imprinting process is, the process of changing our programming by changing the choices we make *is* simple. And yet this step of reprogramming our own minds through the choices we make, adhere to, and demand of ourselves is one of the most effective reprogramming tools that we have ever found.

Choices create change. It's up to *you* to make the choices and this book will show you how.

Angie. And yet this view of Entrepreneurs may own
minds littered and cluttered with more useless mental
lumber in arses to of sales of the these than anyone
together the ...

Clear a defence where it is to travel. with the
mental and the book will show you how

"If you were given only one choice:

∎

<u>*To choose or not to choose,*</u>

∎

Which would you choose?"

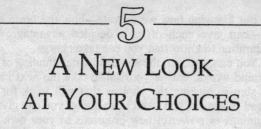

5

A NEW LOOK AT YOUR CHOICES

JUST IMAGINE WHAT making new choices—creating new, positive, powerful self-directed programs—could do in your life.

In the past we learned that it is our programming that affected or controlled the choices we made. It was our programming that stopped us from exercising the free will that was available to us.

It was our programming that set the stage. It gave us the role to play, the costume to wear and, for the most part, the lines of the script that each of us would act out. If we had stopped there you and I would be destined to do nothing more than live out the results of the programming we had received with little or no real control over the outcome of the play.

But now we have learned more. We have learned that our determined choices can, by themselves, affect and change the programming that drives us. What an important discovery that is! That means that each of us has the ability within ourself right now to affect and control an important part of our own future.

It Helps to Know How It Works

If we were not aware of the results of programming in our lives, most of us would be subject to the whims of the world around us without realizing it.

But knowing how we operate—how the *brain* operates—can give each of us a decided advantage. It is exhilarating to know that you can take charge.

You can, by even the simplest understanding of how the mind works, enable yourself to take the next important step in making the choices that will work for you instead of against you. And in so doing, you can give the beginnings of powerful new programs to your own subconscious mind that will turn those choices into reality.

Is this new technique of changing your own programming by making better choices only a "here today, gone tomorrow" notion? Is it the kind of idea that tells you you can reach your loftiest goals, but in the end does nothing more than tell you that you "ought to" do it? Does it leave you hoping for change with no real assurance that the method will work or that it will last?

Making choices is not some "self-help" system. It never has been. *We have always made choices.* But until recently it was not widely recognized that the simple choices we make each day play an amazingly important role in the natural programming processes of the human brain.

Now we have an advantage. Knowledge is on our side. And what we've learned, we can use. Now let's see what we can do with what we have learned.

The First Few Choices Are Just the Beginning

We began our search into the enlightening world of choices with the story of Naci and T'naci. Both of them were given, as a gift from their mother, the opportunity to select their most important choices for themselves.

Naci, as you will recall, used the choices that he was given to create for himself a meaningful and worthwhile life. T'naci, on the other hand, decided to ignore the choices that were in front of him and did not make the choices.

Naci succeeded where T'naci did not. Naci made a

profound difference in his life by deciding to exercise his choices.

But as important as the few simple choices were that Naci chose to make from the cards he was given, they were only the beginning. Each of us has countless choices to make in our lives. Those twelve basic choices that Naci was encouraged to make for himself created for him a foundation on which countless other choices could be built.

If we consciously chose to make those few basic choices, decide for ourselves what we want, how we want to be, who we want to become, and live by those choices, we would give ourselves a foundation that would set us up—program us—to make the *other* choices in life, even the small, day-to-day choices, with the same sense of purpose and direction. That is how choices work.

When we have the major choices under control, we tend to do better with the minor choices that confront us every day. If you take a close look at the major choices in your life, you could very likely figure out what they are and what decisions you should make with each of them.

Suppose you were even more fortunate than Naci and T'naci, and that instead of receiving only twelve cards of choices from someone who cared about you, you were given an almost unlimited list of choices—a list that gave you the opportunity to recognize not twelve but many choices that you could make for yourself.

Naci and T'naci changed their lives and directed their futures with only twelve choices; imagine what you could do if you just as carefully considered even a few dozen of the *other* choices that are available to you— some of them every day. Imagine the effect you could have on your own life, your own future, by being aware of what those choices are, and what *you* choose to do about them.

Here is a list of choices that will get you started. Some of the choices on this list may not apply to you directly, but most of them will. Most of them affect all of us in some manner.

As you read through this list of choices, stop for a moment and consider each of them. Think about each of the choices on this list that could affect you and your life in some way.

Each time you consider this list of choices, you redefine what you want, what you expect, what you hope for, what you believe about yourself, and what you believe about others around you; and you ask yourself to make some decisions.

The choices you make about each of the items on this list will tell you a lot about who you are, what you want, and what you're going to do about it.

A Few of Our Choices

My Education
- I choose to improve my education and learn more in every way I can.
- I choose not to improve my education.

My Family
- I choose to work hard at making my important personal relationships work.
- I choose not to work at making my important relationships work.

My Family
- I choose to do everything I can to make my family the most positive, successful family I can.
- I choose not to work to help my family become the most successful family possible.

My Goals
- I choose to set goals, write them down, work at them, and achieve them.

- I choose not to set goals for myself, and to drift through life without them.

Money
- I choose to believe that I can earn the income and gain the financial freedom that I want.
- I choose not to believe that I can earn the income that I want, and do the things that would lead to my earning it.

My Health
- I choose to be healthy and to do everything I can to keep myself in the best possible physical condition.
- I choose not to be healthy or make the effort to be in the best physical condition that I can.

Exercise
- I choose to exercise regularly.
- I choose not to get regular exercise.

My Job and My Career
- I choose to have a successful, rewarding job or career and to put the necessary effort into this area of my life.
- I choose not to have a successful, rewarding job or career, or to put effort into this area of my life.

How I Enjoy My Work
- I choose to enjoy my work each and every day.
- I choose not to enjoy my work each and every day.

My Talents
- I choose to develop my talents and through my talents create additional benefits in my life.

■ I choose not to develop my talents, but to let them lie dormant without contributing to my life.

My Attitude

■ I choose to have a good attitude. I choose to look at life from the perspective of making things work, and doing everything to see the best in who I am and everything around me.

■ I choose not to have a good attitude. I choose not to look at life from the perspective of making things work, or do anything to see my life and my self at my best.

Fairness

■ I choose to be fair in everything I do.

■ I choose not to be fair in everything I do.

How I Deal With Problems

■ I choose to see problems as normal parts of life. I choose to tackle and deal with problems in a positive and productive way.

■ I choose to see problems as an unnatural and unacceptable part of life, and I choose to be unwilling to give positive energy to solving them.

My Ability To Pay Attention To Others

■ I choose to listen to others, to be interested in what they have to say, to learn from them, and to give them feedback that is useful and worthwhile.

■ I choose not to listen to others or to be interested in what they have to say that might help me learn; and I choose not to respond to their situations.

Learning From Failure

■ I choose to learn from failure and to see failure as a way to increase my skills and understanding.

■ I choose not to learn from failure, but to see it as a pointless defeat.

My Self-Importance

■ I choose to know that I am important, and to believe that what I have to say, think, and do are important, not only for me, but for the people around me. I choose to do this in the most caring, accepting, understanding and nurturing way possible.

■ I choose to see myself as unimportant, and to believe that the things I have to say, think and do are unimportant, not only to me, but to the people around me.

My Ego

■ I choose to see myself and my ego as strong and worthy. I also choose to see my own ego as supportive and helpful to the self-belief of others.

■ I choose to see myself and my ego as weak and unworthy. I also choose to belittle the self-belief of others.

How I Spend My Time

■ I choose to spend my time in ways that contribute to my greatest well-being and the greatest well-being of others.

■ I do not choose to spend my time in ways that contribute to my well-being or to the well-being of others.

My Time For Myself

■ I choose to give myself time to do the things I want to do, and to give myself the space to create and replenish the best of myself.

■ I choose not to give myself time to do the things I want to do or those things that replenish and strengthen me.

My Productivity

- I choose to make my life productive and useful, and to do things that improve my life and the lives of others.
- I choose not to make my life useful or productive, or to do anything to improve my life or the lives of others.

How I Care

- I choose to care about others, to recognize that I care about them and to show my caring in the things that I do.
- I choose not to care about others or do anything that would make them think I care.

My Consideration

- I choose to be considerate of others and to always take the time and effort to understand who they are, their goals and their objectives.
- I choose not to bother with being considerate of others or to try to understand them.

My Friendliness

- I choose to be friendly, open, and warm toward others.
- I choose not to be friendly but to close myself off from others.

My Belief In Others

- I choose to believe in others and to show them that belief in ways that will help them to believe in themselves.
- I choose not to believe in others, or to let them think that their self-belief has any validity.

My Feelings About Giving

- I choose to give, and to do so in such a way that the greatest possible good is created from what I have to offer.

■ I choose not to give of myself or my possessions, or to care about what could be accomplished if I did give.

My Feelings About Receiving—Accepting From Others

■ I choose to accept openly and thankfully what others have to offer me, and I choose to always let them know my appreciation for who they are and what they do.

■ I choose not to gracefully accept what others have to offer me, or to care how they feel about my response.

My Abilities As a Parent

■ I choose to be the very best parent that I can possibly be. I choose to give love, nurturing, teaching, understanding, care, acceptance and belief.

■ I choose not to be a good parent and I choose not to care about what is going on in the lives, minds and hearts of my children.

My Friendship

■ I choose to be a good friend. As a good friend I choose to always work to understand, support, and bring out the very best in others.

■ I choose not to be a good friend, but to get whatever I can out of friendships and give as little in return as I can get by with.

My Financial Responsibility

■ I choose to be financially responsible. I choose to take care of every financial responsibility I have *on time*.

■ I choose to be financially irresponsible. I choose to live a life dodging those I owe and never feeling the satisfaction of knowing that I'm square with the world.

My Appearance

- I choose to look good, and to present myself in the most attractive and personable way that I can.

- I choose not to look good, but to turn others away from me because of my appearance.

The Way I Talk To Others

- I choose to always express myself in a way that communicates my thoughts and allows others to see the very best in me.

- I choose to talk without thinking about whether my words reflect what I'm thinking and trying to communicate, or whether my speech speaks well for and of me.

The Way I Talk To Myself

- I choose to tell myself and direct my mind with only those thoughts and directions which work *for* me, to the greatest possible good.

- I choose to talk to myself in a way that is cluttered, not directed, and mostly negative.

That list of choices could go on indefinitely. Those are simple choices, and there are thousands of them in our lives. But the list gives you the idea. How often do we really sit down and think about some of the most basic and yet most important choices of our lives?

When it comes down to it, it isn't the major choices we make in life—career, marriage, etc.—that count the most. It is the everyday, *minor* decisions like those we have just reviewed, and countless others, that make life work for us.

And yet we all too often think about these choices only when they present themselves in such a way that we are forced to deal with them. Even then we seldom recognize that they are *choices*.

I have known people who have literally changed their lives because of making the decision to make conscious choices in even one or two areas. I've known people who have made the conscious choices to "like their jobs"—and because of that one simple choice things went better each day at work.

I have known others who have sat down, thought about it, and made the simple choice to spend more time with their families. The result of that one simple choice was a not only noticeable, but nearly overwhelming, change in their family lives.

We all have known people who have made the decision to change something, to fix something in their lives, to believe in their decision strongly enough to do something about it, and then to see the change take place.

With all the potentially negative programs working against them, why did those individuals successfully create the change? It was because they made a simple decision, *chose* to make the choice work, and acted on it.

Choosing to Override Past Programs

You can, if you choose, override your past programming by *choice*. Countless individuals just like you and me have overcome what would have seemed insurmountable odds and have come out winning simply because they chose to do so.

Old programs may stand in your way when you decide to choose. But your choice—your strong, determined choice—is in itself a program that has exceptional power and strength in the chemistry of the mind.

Would you like to be happier tomorrow? Choose to be happier tomorrow. Would you like to get along better with your teenage son or daughter? *Choose* to get along better. Do everything it takes to reach your objective, and watch what happens.

Would you like to be more successful as a salesperson and reach your objective to make more sales, starting now? *Choose* to do it, and watch what happens. Would you like to get yourself in better shape, lose weight, and keep the weight off? *Choose* to do it.

Override the old programming that told you that you could not get along with the teenage son or daughter. Override the old programming that told you that you were destined to be overweight. *Choose* to override the old program that told you that you could not be Number One in sales.

And then, every day, from here on out, give yourself that same new program that tells you what you *can* do instead of accepting the old programs that convinced you that you could not.

Make the choice. Not just once, but every moment of every day. Keep making the choice. Give yourself a nonstop mental diet of positive, powerful programs of choice.

In the past, when you have allowed your own programming to take off on its own, the best you could do is hope for fortune or luck to be on your side now and then. But that's not how the brain works.

If you'd like to take control, *take control*. Make your choices. Know what they are. Write them down. Read them and reread them.

In the past, the influences of the world have programmed, directed and controlled the best of us. It's time we took charge of the best of ourselves.

Define your choices. Decide for yourself what you want, how you want to live and who you want to be. Give *that* program to your brain, deliver *that* kind of specific, strong self-direction to your subconscious mind beginning today and continuing tomorrow and every day thereafter. And then stand back and watch what happens.

Your own brain will do for you what you tell it to do, as long as you get your messages across. And some of the strongest messages you ever give to yourself will be the messages you give in the choices you make.

"The choices we make by accident are just as important as the choices we make by design."

CONSCIOUS CHOICES —CLEAR RESULTS

THE PRINCIPAL REASON why we fail to make many of the choices we should be making is that we fail to recognize them as choices in the first place.

Because of the programming we receive, it is entirely possible to grow up almost unaware that if we're not making choices for ourselves, we are then living out the results of the programming we receive from others. We are not thinking for ourselves. Others are doing it for us.

Thinking for Yourself

Have you ever wondered why there is so little true "original" thinking done? It isn't because there is no need for original thinking; quite the opposite. What this world *needs* right now are some original, new solutions. It isn't because we're incapable of original thought.

Almost any of us, with a little coaching, can come up with thoughts and ideas that are genuinely new and creative. Why do business colleges have to teach creative thinking to adult businesspeople? After all, we are all born naturally creative.

I know people who can go through an entire day without having a single original thought. I know mature, adult men and women of incredible potential who can go entire days or weeks without ever having to think for themselves.

I know others who go through an entire lifetime believing that making choices is nothing more than selecting which color dress or what tie to wear to work that day.

The fact is, we are taught "not to think." We're not taught this directly, of course, by our parents or by our teachers at school. We are taught it indirectly, through countless thousands of programs that are given to us day after day, year after year, that create within us an internal picture of ourselves, *relying on the choices of others*.

In time, with enough of this kind of programming in place in our subconscious mind, we actually come to believe that it's okay to follow the crowd, and go along with what's happening.

Or, at another level, we come to believe that it's normal and natural for us to accept the pictures and descriptions of us that we now hold as our self-identity in our subconscious mind, with no regard for the fact that those pictures of ourselves may be entirely inaccurate.

But our programming tells us to go along with whatever is there. "Don't try to be any different," it tells us. "This is how you are. This is how you were meant to be." And if that means that you are destined to live out a life that is unfulfilling or unrewarding, full of problems and personal woes, just get used to it, your subconscious mind tells you, after all, that is how you are.

What Happens to the Potential That Could Have Been?

Let's take for example a young man who is about to be married. He was average in school, spent little time thinking about his future and less time setting goals. He did not prepare himself with the kind of education he could have gotten if he had tried. He has never paid particularly close attention to how he looks and is little concerned with how the rest of the world sees him.

He spends three to four evenings a week sitting in front of the television set, and some time with his friends from work. And because he has a reasonably good job, he's not too concerned about his future, or the future of his new family.

There may be nothing "wrong" with his life—but neither will he reach more than a fraction of the potential he was born with. All in all he is unremarkable, 100 percent the product of his programming.

What kind of choices do you suppose this young man will make as he grows older, takes on the responsibilities of a family, and works his way through the rest of his life?

How many of this man's choices do you suppose will genuinely be his own? Most of his choices will be made without his ever thinking about it. They will be unconscious. They will be the product of the programming that put him there.

But even if we used as our example a young man or woman who was *above* average, the problem would be much the same. Unless we *think*, clearly and consciously, about each and every choice we make, our choices will *always* be made for us by someone else or by the programs that we carry with us in our subconscious minds.

It is only when we have worked to change those programs of the mind, through our own self-directed Self-Talk, that we can begin to rely on those programs in making our choices and decisions for us.

Until then, we'll have to do our thinking for ourselves. If we want to make a good choice, we'll have to *think* about it. Sometimes, we'll have to think long and hard.

Sometimes we'll have to think the same choice through time and time again, looking at it from every angle, until we're absolutely sure that we're making the best possible choice.

Getting to that point, the point at which we are

consciously thinking through each of our choices each day, may not always be easy.

Why? Our old programs, the same programs that are often giving us the wrong information on which to base choices, don't want us to think.

Those old programs tell us: "Do it my way. Do it the old way. Why should you change now? Why should you start thinking for yourself now? After all," the old programs of the subconscious mind say, you've always let me make your choices for you in the past; why would you want to make your choices for yourself now?"

The Importance of Conscious Choices

If you want to make better choices, why do your choices now have to be conscious choices? So you will *think* about them.

It is by choice of *will,* your own will now overriding your old programming, that you can finally set the record straight, make the right choices for you today, and in so doing set up a *pattern* of choices that begin to create new, more positive, more productive programs in your subconscious mind:

- Our identity and our beliefs are programmed into us from birth.
- As much as three-fourths of all our programming is negative or the wrong kind.
- Our unconscious choices are made for us by the programs we carry in our minds.
- The choices we make unconsciously can be no better than the programs behind them.
- Taking conscious control over each choice interrupts and stops the old programs from creating poor choices.
- New, *conscious* choices create strong, new, more powerful and more accurate programs in the subconscious mind.

Until recently, when we began to understand more of the workings of the subconscious mind, we did not know that letting our choices and decisions passively come and go was causing a much bigger problem than just ending up with bad choices.

We did not know that making choices consciously is one of the strongest ways we have ever found to override poor programming and put strong, healthier, new programs in their place.

The Clearer the Picture—the Better the Choice

If you were to look at an entire list made up of "Who are you and what do you want?" there are sure to be a lot of items on that list that you deserve to have in your life. And getting them will depend on the choices you make. So you can imagine what you might end up with if your choices are unclear, cloudy, or vague.

People who have unclear goals, unclear pictures of themselves, and make unclear choices, end up with an unclear future—and never a *chance* at reaching what they thought they had wanted.

This process of consciously thinking clearly through each and every choice you make is closely related to the concept of creating more energy by crystallizing your attention and focusing your goals. The more attention and concentration you give to anything, the more energy will go along with that attention. If your choices are clear, concentrated and precise, you will automatically give more energy to making those choices work.

Most of us are aware of family members or friends who are not even aware that they are making choices. They are making the choices, of course, but they are making them unconsciously.

And without knowing they're making the choices in the first place, they would certainly have no way of knowing their choices are being made for them by subconscious programs which may be exactly the *wrong* programs to make the *right* choices.

How *do* you become aware of the choices you make? How do you recognize choices which in the past were unconscious, and bring them out into the daylight where you can see them, examine them, think about them, and put yourself in charge of them?

How do you cast your personal ballot for the choices that will be in your best interest?

Every time you make an *unconscious choice*, something within you is doing the voting *for* you. Let's see how it works.

"Another person's choice is nothing more than another alternative for you to consider."

7

WHO'S DOING
THE VOTING?

THE WAY IN WHICH CHOICES are made in the brain is very complex. What we refer to simply as the process of "making choices" is, in fact, an extremely complicated self-management guidance system. It is an incredibly sophisticated information gathering, storing, and retrieval system utilizing a network of 15 billion to 100 billion neurons in the brain.

The Powerful "Computer" of Your Brain

This system chemically and electrically receives information about us and everything we perceive about us, categorizes the information, and files it. In turn, this information system directs a massively powerful electrochemical computer-like control center which sends millions of messages to our physiological and psychological operating systems. Those millions of messages to and from our control center are what activate and operate us. And every message—every piece of information the brain receives—is treated not just as one choice, but as an almost infinite number of choices. As the brain receives each message, it sorts through its countless files of preprogrammed directions and stored information. It then determines what to do about each piece of information it receives that could affect us in any way.

You Don't Have to Think About It—but It Helps

Fortunately, we don't have to be aware of most of what is going on in the decision-making process in the brain. The brain is designed to handle most of its tens of thousands of unconscious daily choices almost entirely by itself.

But what you think about the conscious choices of which you *are* aware helps your brain do its job better. That means that your brain will be able to make choices that work more in your favor, more to your liking, and give you more moments and hours and days of living better and feeling better about yourself in the process.

Let's take a look upstairs in the computer control center of the subconscious mind. If we could picture a slow-motion, imaginary sequence of what happens when we ask the brain to make a decision for us, it might look something like this:

Imagine that we are standing in the part of the subconscious mind where all of our past programming is stored. Wall after wall of this huge storage center is covered with filing cabinets from floor to ceiling.

In those storage cabinets are stored the hundreds of thousands—the millions—of programs we have been given over the years, and the millions more we have given ourselves through our own internal Self-Talk.

In the center of this control center let us say that there is a computer screen, and it is flashing a message. The message asks us to make a decision. Since this is an unconscious decision and one that we're not going to think about, in this case the decision is going to be made automatically. The subconscious mind will handle most of the decision-making process all by itself without our conscious help.

When the request for the decision flashes on the computer screen, the automatic process of the control center immediately begins sorting through the appropriate banks of files—thousands of them.

It is what is stored in those files that will tell the control center what decision it should recommend. File after file of related information is sorted and sifted through. Every piece of stored information that could affect that decision in any way is analyzed at lightning speed.

File by file, page by page, the vote begins to come in; the decision is taking shape. Each piece of information stored in those files adds to the vote. And then, because of the incredible speed of this powerful computer-like process of the subconscious mind, the decision is made. The vote is in and the decision is ready to be handed down.

Sometimes we are notified of the vote consciously; sometimes we are not aware at all that the vote was taken and the decision was made. We have just made another choice without even thinking about it.

We hope, of course, that it was a good choice. We hope that the files in our minds contained enough of the right information to make a good choice. But if the files hold the wrong information—that which is negative or could in some way work against us, based on negative or inaccurate beliefs that have been stored there in our past—then the decision that was made, in all likelihood will be the wrong decision.

Let's say the decision we're discussing is taking place in the mind of a seventeen-year-old high-school student. Doug is walking to school and is about to step from the street onto the sidewalk in front of the school. It is just five minutes before his first class.

At that moment a car loaded with Doug's friends screeches up to the curb and his friends yell out, telling Doug to cut class with them that day. Doug turns toward the car. The door handle is less than four feet away, and as he turns, he starts to reach for that handle . . . and then, for only a moment, hesitates.

In that instant a question is flashed across the master

video screen in the computer control center of his brain. Before Doug has even had time to think consciously about it, the question is there: "OKAY TO SKIP SCHOOL?"

In that same instant *thousands* of file drawers in Doug's computer control center are flying open at lightning speed. File after file that stores Doug's programs about school; schoolwork; teachers; parents; college; grades; his girlfriend; the opinions of his peer group; past successes and failures in school; rights; wrongs; the importance of personal responsibility; and a huge bank of files that make up his self-esteem *all vote!* File after file, program after program, vote—and in that same moment, the vote is in.

On the master video screen in Doug's computer control center the answer flashes on the screen: "GO AHEAD. OKAY TO SKIP SCHOOL."

The question was asked, the programs searched, the vote taken, and the answer was in, all before Doug could reach the door handle, open the car door, and jump in. Did he really make a *conscious* choice? Who did the voting? Was it *Doug*, or was it the programs he had stored in his subconscious mind?

Unconscious Choices Are Always the Result of the Programs That Are Doing the Voting

What really happened in that unconscious control center is that of all the thousands of mental files that were quickly examined, *most* of them were files that voted in favor of skipping school: *Thousands* of files of influence from friends, other files of attitudes about school, and a host of files having to do with peer group pressure, and going along with the crowd, files of how he felt about his parents, a huge section of files that make up his self-esteem, and his sense of personal responsibility. Good or bad, all got together and cast the deciding vote.

The young man made the choice without *really* making the choice for himself, and without even being aware of the incredible process in his mind that ended up making the choice for him.

Let's look at another example. A woman who wants to lose thirty pounds and has spent several years trying to take the weight off and keep it off, is unsuccessfully on another diet. She is out with a group of friends from the office, having lunch, and she has successfully managed to eat only a small portion of what she ordered.

Then, in the middle of a conversation with her friends, without even thinking about it, she picks up her fork. She is about to make an unconscious decision: to eat more, or to stick to her diet.

Upstairs in the computer control center in her subconscious mind, a message is flashed on the computer screen. The message reads, "OKAY TO EAT THIS EXTRA BITE?"

In less than a moment the subconscious mind goes to work sorting and searching through file after file of every piece of information the young lady has stored about herself, her eating habits, her appearance, her frustrations, her rewards, and her many past failures in dieting along the way.

In that moment, based on what she has already stored in her files, the vote is taken, and the decision is flashed on her computer control screen: "GO AHEAD."

Then there is the man who wakes up to the first sound of the buzz of his alarm. He had promised himself faithfully the night before that he was going to get up early and take care of some paperwork that he knew he had to complete before he left for the office this morning. In an instant his control center is rapidly, silently, examining the files.

The files it selects are the man's programs of past performance: how he feels about his work, how he sees himself—as an achiever or someone who can just "get by," and countless programs of pictures of himself either getting things done or putting them off.

Before the man can even reach to push the button on top of the alarm clock that turns it off, the vote in his subconscious control center has already been taken, and the answer instantly appears on the computer control screen: "IT'S OKAY, DON'T GET UP," and his hand instead reaches for the other button on the alarm clock that resets it to wake him again later. Once again, unconscious choices are always voted on by the overriding programs we have stored in our subconscious minds.

And this is why, without knowing it, we so often make decisions that work against us instead of for us. If as much as 75 percent of the programming we received from others and then learned to give to ourselves through our Self-Talk is negative, or works against us, then we must recognize that when the vote is taken—unconsciously—as much as 75 percent of the votes will be *against* us instead of *for* us.

What a powerful influence our own programming plays in our lives. But *knowing* that, gives us a tremendous advantage. Imagine what our unconscious choices would be if we gave ourselves better programs to work with. Imagine having files of the mind that are so clearly programmed in our behalf that every time the vote was taken—or at least most of the time—we would make the very best possible choice.

Override Your Old Programming with the Choices You Make Today

It is a marvelous faculty of the human mind that we are also able to stop old programming from holding us back, anytime we choose to. That gift is called *conscious choice*.

Most of us have enough files in our mind—plenty of them—that we can call up to support us when we want to override an old program and make a better decision. When the question comes up, when the choice is flashed on our computer control screen we can step in, take control and say: "HOLD IT! I'm in charge here! Now let's find the programs that help me win!"

If you ask it, that same subconscious control center

will search through its files and present you with all the information you need to help you make the right decision for yourself.

It's very likely that the teenage student who cut classes with his friends had enough of the *other* kinds of files, ready to help him make the *right* decision, the right choice, if only he had asked.

The businessman who slept through his goal to get something done *could* have, if he had thought about it, called on the best of his programming to see himself as a strong, capable professional, and given himself the right choice.

By allowing her hidden programs to make her decision for her, the young woman at lunch overlooked the powerful potential that her mind had to help her exercise better judgment at the moment, and push the plate away.

That's how the mind works. If we understand it, and learn to use it *for* us, we learn to take control over the resources of our mind. It will do anything we ask to give us our best and to help us make the choices we so badly want to make.

Of course, the actual physiological electrochemical function of the brain is far more complex than the simple picture of the subconscious control center that we've just talked about.

That seemingly simple process that the brain goes through to make choices for us, or to wait for us to tell it what choices we really want to make, is actually made up of billions of circuits in the brain, electrochemical switches and pathways, and an information storage and retrieval center that is so overwhelmingly complex that we are just now starting to understand how it operates.

But we have now learned enough about the brain to know how to treat it and direct it. We've learned more about how to help our own brain direct its tremendous computer-like energy to work *for* us, by listening carefully for every choice we want to make, and making sure that each of those choices is the correct choice.

You Can Do Your Voting
for Yourself

Because those new choices become new programs in the subconscious mind, that same brain will also work tirelessly to take action on those choices.

If we tell our mind what to do, strongly enough, often enough, and clearly enough, it will do everything it can to make it happen.

Ask yourself the questions: *"Who is voting on my decisions? What programs do I have in my subconscious mind right now that I'm allowing to make my decisions for me?"*

Wouldn't you rather cast the deciding vote *yourself?* If you do not take an active role in casting your vote—in making the choice *consciously* for yourself—the programs in your mind will do the voting for you. Some of them will vote for you and give you choices that are worthwhile and productive. Many of them will not.

If you were raised to have strong programs of self-belief, self-esteem, personal responsibility, and positive, workable attitudes about everything you do in life, you can count on much of your programming to serve you well.

But if you, like most of us, received along the way too many of those programs that taught us to believe less in ourselves, reduced our self-esteem, took away our personal responsibility, and gave us questionable attitudes about life, then it will always be up to you to change those programs or override them by your choice.

You have so much potential. But it will always be up to you to look for it, find it, and, through your own *conscious* choices, give it life.

*"There is no life as complete
as the life that is lived
by choice."*

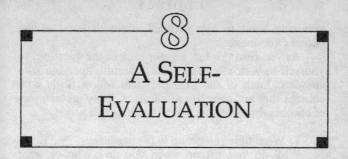

8

A SELF-
EVALUATION

IN AN EARLIER CHAPTER we asked the question, "Who are you and what do you want?" The answer to that question plays an unbelievably important role in every choice you will ever make.

One of the best ways to learn the answer to that question is to find out where you stand on some of the basic choices that you make, either consciously or unconsciously, and act on them in some way each and every day.

Let's look at a list of just a few examples of some of the choices that are affecting you right now. This list could include *hundreds* of examples of choices that you and I deal with every day, but I've selected a few examples of the choices we make that give us a direct insight into who we *really* are and what we *really* want.

It isn't always easy to find out who, in the most realistic and practical way, you would really most like to be, or what you truly want out of life. But each time you evaluate the choices you make, ask yourself the questions and give yourself clear answers. You will learn more.

The list of examples I've selected for this self-evaluation is not the final list. The final list could go on indefinitely. But it will give you an idea of the questions you may want to ask yourself about the rest of the choices you make.

As you read this list, answer each of the questions to yourself in your mind, and listen carefully for your own answers. Each of the examples that follow deals with choices that are common to all of us. They are samples of choices that affect us every day in untold ways:

1. What time you get up in the morning.

Why do you get up when you do? Who or what determines the time you wake up each morning and get started with your day? Are you getting up each day at the time you like to, or if you could change it (realistically) would you?

How much choice do you feel you have in the matter of when you get up? Do you feel you are in control of the start of each day? Are you getting up when you should? Do you want to make a change in the time you get up each day—a time that would fit the schedule that *you* would like to create for yourself?

A number of years ago, during the time when I was first spending "extra" time each day to write the word-for-word Self-Talk scripts for cassette recordings, I came across the surprising statistic that if you get up just one hour earlier each morning you will add the equivalent of over *two* additional months of productive work days each year. I was so impressed with the idea that I got out my calculator to see if it was true—and it was.

Knowing that I had a lot of writing to accomplish I decided to double the effect and wake myself *two* hours earlier each morning and devote that quiet, uninterrupted time to writing the Self-Talk scripts before I began my regular work schedule each day.

To do that, I had to make a major choice. And I had to follow up that choice with a great deal of self-discipline in order to get up at 4 o'clock each morning. But eventually I got used to the new schedule, and it worked.

I remember thinking at the time how easy it is for each of us to get trapped into the schedules that are imposed upon us by the rest of the world. I am not suggesting in any way that you get up a moment earlier, or later, each day than you choose to. After all, all of us ought to make sure that we get the healthy amount of rest and sleep that suits us best.

But I am suggesting that you reread the questions above and *determine whether you are setting the schedule of your life based on the expectations of others or by the expectations of your own choices.* This is one of the most important facts you can learn; the schedule you have set by your own personal choice.

2. Your personal appearance.

How do you look? How do you *want* to look? Have you positioned yourself and your appearance in a way that clearly maximizes the opportunity for reaching your objectives—both personally and professionally?

Are you satisfied with your figure or physique? If it is naturally and biologically helpful to do something about it—are you? How would you like the world to perceive you? Is that the way you are?

Or do you need some extra work and attention in your personal appearance? When you look in the mirror do you feel good about yourself? Does the way you look detract from your self-esteem, or add to it?

We present, and the world perceives. Like it or not, everyone around us draws their own conclusions from the appearance we present. No matter how hard we try or what steps we take, we cannot always change the size and the shape of what our ancestors handed down to us. But it is always an individual choice to make the best of what we've got. What you do with what you've got is your choice. It is always up to you.

3. Your job, career, or position in life.

What powerful forces come into play in this one example of personal choice! Are you in the job or profession that you want to be in? Are you happy with your chosen career? Do you stay with it and enjoy it, or do you stay with it and complain?

Do you feel that it was your choice to be where you are, or do you feel the choice was made by the expectations of someone else? Are you giving it all you've got? Do you plan to make a change? If you could do it all over again, would you do the same?

I was amazed to read the statistic years ago that as many as 85 percent of the people in jobs five years after completing school were no longer happy with the profession or the job they had chosen. If that statistic is even close to being correct, then it is no wonder that so many people seem to be frustrated about their jobs.

It is also no wonder that so many individuals are frustrated about their work because they feel that it "had to be that way." All too many of them feel that when it came right down to it, they had no choice.

The truth is that we *always* have a choice in every career decision we make, every step of the way. Those among us who recognize that fact and finally make the decision to start making *choices,* can't wait to tell you how their lives changed when they finally found the freedom to make choices in their lives.

If you're doing what you want to be doing, keep doing it. *Enjoy it!* If you're not doing what you truly want to be doing, make a choice.

4. Your personal style—the way you deal with others.

Are you happy with the way you get along with others? Are you happy with the way people treat you in return? Do you do the things you need to do to present to others the best that you have to offer? Are you a good listener? Do you care, and do you show it when you do? Do you talk, speak and present your ideas the way you'd like to?

Do you let your emotions override your better judgment, or do you keep your emotions in check? Do you let yourself say things that you wish later you had not said? Do you help others see themselves in the best possible way?

Do you create arguments, or do you defuse them? Do people respect you for the way you treat *them*? Are your relationships in general, at home, at work, with friends, etc., living up to what you would like them to be? Do you make conscious choices about your personal style and the way you deal with others?

Most of us have heard someone say at one time or another, ''Well, that's just the way I am.'' When someone says that, what he is really saying is, ''That's the way my *programming* taught me to be, and *I* don't have any choice in the matter.''

Do they have any choice in the matter? Of course they do. Each of us has an almost unlimited amount of choice, in the determination of how we get along with others, in what our style is, and in how to improve that style anytime we choose.

The way you get along with others is not an accident—it is *always* a choice. It is entirely up to you. None of us was born with manners, style, attitudes, or ''people skills.'' We learned them. They are a part of our programs. And any of us, if we choose, can change the programs that work against us and replace them with new programs that work *for* us.

If you have a style that is working against you, make a choice. Change it. If you have a style that is working for you, make a choice—keep doing it.

5. How you deal with problems.

Do problems get you down, or do they get you moving? Do you hate to see the next problem arise, or do you look at it matter-of-factly as a ''fact of life''?

Do you look for and find the *opportunities* that many problems hold within them? Do you choose to see problems as ''stepping stones to success,'' or impossible obstacles that hold you back and get you nowhere? If you could, would you choose to avoid problems altogether?

Do you give yourself the courage, confidence and self-conviction to tackle any problem facing you?

The way you look at problems will always be a matter of personal choice. We all have problems, yet sometimes we struggle so fiercely to avoid them.

It is unfortunate that most of us have learned to believe that the word "problem" represents only the bramble bush and none of the roses. I will never forget the friend who once told me, "Problems are no problem! I can handle them!" That was his choice. It was an exceptional choice.

6. Your goal-setting skills.

Do you choose to set goals? How often? Do you write them down? Are your goals *specific* goals? Do you define them, give yourself a precise timetable to follow and write it on the calendar? Do you clearly define the results you expect to get?

It would be impossible to overstate the value of setting good goals. It has been said that less than 3 percent of the people around us ever set detailed goals for each area of their lives, write them down, review them, and follow the plan.

It is no surprise we are also told that only 3 percent of those around us acknowledge they are reaching the level of fulfillment that they had wanted to attain in their lives.

Setting specific goals is a choice. Acting on those goals every day is a choice. And living out the positive results—receiving the rewards—is also a choice.

7. Choosing your friends.

Do you choose your friends? Do you surround yourself with the kinds of people you respect most? Do your friends build you up, or do they hold you down? Which of your friends are really friends?

Given the choice, with whom would you choose to spend your time? (That *is* always your choice.) Do you genuinely like the people you call your friends? Are there others with whom you would like to make friends, but have not taken the time to do so?

If you were to write a list of the names of the people with whom you would most like to spend your time (if it were practical), what names would be on that list?

We are influenced by the friendships we keep—negatively or positively. Our own incredibly receptive subconscious minds are always open and listening to every word, every moment of input.

We have all known someone whose "best friend"—because of a negative attitude, poorly programmed self-belief, and an unfulfilled picture of life—was no real friend at all. We find these friends around us at work, in our neighborhoods, at church, and at school.

Choose your friends well. Select them carefully. Whether you have a lot of friends or a few, they play an important role in the influences that create the picture of who you see yourself to be.

We all choose a certain amount of time that we devote to developing and maintaining the friendships we have. When you choose to give your time away to someone else, make sure it is time well spent.

8. How you spend your spare time.

You have in front of you an infinite number of ways to spend every moment of the spare time that you have available to you. What do you do with it? Do you spend your spare time by your choice or do you spend it by the choice of someone else? Do you share your spare time wisely?

If you could spend your spare time differently, what would you do? Do you feel that you are consciously in control of the extra time you have or does it just "happen"? Do you feel that your spare time is lost time, or some of the most valuable time you have?

I've heard people say, "I just don't have enough time," or, "I'm too busy to get anything done," or, "I wish I had more time."

I have also heard people say, "I'm bored, I have

nothing to do," or, "I just don't know what to do with my time." In both cases the missing ingredient is the exercise of choice.

From the day you set out on your own to build a life for yourself, to the moment you breathe your final breath of life, you have two basic gifts to use throughout your life. One of them is your mind—and what you do with it. The other is your personal time and energy—and what you do with them.

It is unfortunate that so many of us come to believe, because of our past programming, that our time is not our own. It *is* our own. It belongs to each of us! What you do with your time is always ultimately up to you.

If you believe that your time is overfilled with obligations, who do you suppose sets or accepts your obligations? It is always you. It is always your choice. If you find yourself immediately saying, "But I have to do this . . ." or, "I have to do that . . ." ask yourself the question, "Whose choice is it?" In this enlightened day and age, you are owned by no one. Neither is your time.

9. Your level of education.

How much do you know? How much more would you like to know? How do you feel about learning more? What do you do about it? How do you stimulate your mind? Are you genuinely "aware," or do you choose not to be? Have you consciously chosen the level of knowledge you would like to attain?

The attainment of knowledge is always a choice—though for many, an unconscious choice. It is unfortunate that many people are taught to believe that "education" ends with formal education. But when it comes to learning, there is an undeniable fact: Given a healthy attitude and a good working mind, the more you know, the better you're able to do.

How many problems we place on ourselves because of something we did not know! A curious, inquisitive, eager mind is a healthy and fertile field. More good things grow better there. How fertile would you like your field

to be? How full and complete and rich a life would
like to live?

Wanting to learn is a choice. It is a benefit of the
society we live in today, that there is virtually no one
who cannot in some way choose to learn something more,
something valuable, something useful, if he or she
chooses to do so. There are bookstores, libraries, computers, seminars and an endless list of available classes
at schools and colleges. The decision to learn is a choice,
and it is a decision that each of us can make.

10. What you expect from yourself.

What *do* you expect from yourself? All the examples
of the choices we have discussed in this chapter are
important, but this choice—what you expect from yourself—is almost without peer. It asks you to make choices
that get to the very root of your self-esteem, who you
are, and what you most expect from yourself.

This one choice confronts you with that one important question: *Who are you, and what do you want?* All
the choices we make, when combined, lead us to the
answer.

Do you expect great things from yourself? Do you
choose to "get by," "get along," and just "hang in there
as long as you can"? Do you expect yourself to be better
than average, or not? Would you like to live out more of
the potential you were *born* to achieve?

Sometime, when you have the time, sit down by
yourself in a quiet place and ask yourself the question,
"What do I really expect from myself?" And then listen
for your answers.

It is this one question more than any other that asks
you to come face to face with what you are doing with
the life you were given. What you answer—and what you
choose to do about it—could make a profound difference
on the time you have left.

This is the question—the choice—that will affect and
direct *every other choice* you will ever make. I have

known people who have asked themselves this question but have never really taken the time to find the answer.

When that happens, it is always unfortunate. You cannot possibly direct your life in the most meaningful way without coming to grips with what you're doing here in the first place, what you expect of yourself, and what you plan to do about it.

This may not be an easy choice, but never ignore it. Figure out for yourself who you are. Decide what you want. Come to terms with your personal meaning and value in life.

The choice that asks you to determine what you expect for yourself is not some lofty, philosophical perspective of who you are. It is down to earth, practical, realistic and day-to-day. It governs everything about you. And looking for, finding, and making the right choices about what you *expect* from yourself will give you a freedom that few individuals ever hope to achieve.

Those are just a few examples of the many that we live with every day, whether we think about it or not. They may appear to be exceptionally important choices, but then if you think about it, most of our choices are important. Our choices affect us, they direct us, they program us, and they influence everything we say and do every day of our lives.

But most important, those few examples underscore the importance of taking control of our own lives through the choices we make. Some who read this and understand it will apply the concept of making choices to their everyday lives. Others will not.

I suspect that those who do, will in many ways live a better life because they made the one simple decision to consciously, actively make choices. They will have made the one single most important choice that any of us could ever make. They will have armed themselves with one of the most effective and lasting self-programming and self-management tools that we have ever found. They will have made the choice to make choices.

*"There may be a thousand
little choices in a day.*

■

All of them count."

9

YOUR ONE HUNDRED
MOST IMPORTANT
CHOICES

WHEN WE BEGIN TO TAKE a careful look at the choices we make, it's easy to come to the conclusion that our most important choices are the choices that guide and direct the major areas of our life.

It is easy to think that if we make good choices about our career, marriage, education, income, family, etc., we should be able to do just fine.

But what about the *other* choices—the thousands of almost unnoticed choices that all of us make (or do not make), day in and day out? How important *are* those "little" choices?

They are exceptionally important. It may be the big choices in life that set the direction for where we're going, but it is the little choices that get us there.

Our loftiest goals become nothing more than unfulfilled dreams that fall by the wayside if we do not just as carefully *make*, and *act on* the smaller choices along the way. What do the little choices look like? I'll give you some examples.

Here is a list of 100 choices. Some of them seem important; others seem so insignificant that we might wonder how they could be important at all. But each of them makes up some part of what we call "life."

As you read through this list, notice that any one of the choices, no matter how seemingly insignificant, affects something about us; what we do, how we spend our time, what we think and how we think, how we feel, what we like or dislike, what works for us and what does not.

Each of us makes tens of thousands of choices in a lifetime. Here are just a few of them:

- Who you spend most of your time with
- How you comb your hair
- What your favorite foods are
- What you eat most often
- How often you call home
- The books you read
- Your posture
- How much or how little you smile
- What you watch on television and how much you watch
- Your hobbies
- How much you exercise
- Whether you argue more than you should
- The style and color clothes you wear
- Who you invite to a party
- Whether you write letters
- Which telephone calls you return
- The appearance of your home
- How long something stays broken before you fix it
- How late you stay up at night
- What time you get up in the morning
- How well you listen to others
- Whether you smoke
- Whether you gossip
- How well you are able to concentrate
- The political candidates you vote for
- Whether you like or fear computers
- How fast you drive
- How much risk you are willing to take
- Whether you save money
- Whether you are a leader or a follower

- The amount of time you spend with your kids
- How organized you are
- Whether you go to church
- Whether you belong to a social or service organization
- How often you change shoes
- Who you admire most
- How often you are late for something
- What you do about a traffic ticket
- Who pays the bills in your household
- Who decides what to have for dinner
- How much time you give yourself to get ready in the morning
- What you do at the end of the day
- What you drink, if, and how much
- Where you buy your groceries, and why
- How calm you are
- Whose opinions you ask for
- How you handle problems at work
- Whether you attend concerts or cultural events
- How often you eat out
- How interested you are in other people
- How you show your emotions
- What newspapers or magazines you read
- Whether you give free advice
- What kind of car you drive, and what shape it's in
- How you react to negative attitudes or opinions from others
- What sports you participate in
- How you spend your holidays
- How important it is for you to follow the trend
- How much time you spend talking to your spouse or mate
- How important you feel you are
- How you use credit cards
- How you look at problems in the past
- How you treat or relate to members of the opposite sex
- How often you feel sorry for yourself

- Who upsets you the most
- Whether you like a challenge
- Who controls the conversation
- How you feel about world problems
- What you think about while you're getting ready in the morning
- How much you worry
- How much patience you have
- How many compliments you give
- What gets you angry
- How often you almost run out of gas in the car
- What you do when you don't get your way
- How much you spend, and on what
- How often you criticize
- How happy you are
- How you feel about what other people think of you
- How often you do not tell the truth, and why
- How you take care of yourself
- How much you respect yourself
- How often you complain
- How often you have to be reminded of something
- Who you talk to when you have a problem
- How you leave your desk or work space at the end of the day
- What movies you attend
- How often you get a haircut
- How often you have friends visit
- How much encouragement you give to others
- How polite you are
- When you do your Christmas shopping
- What you think about, when you have time to think
- How much time you take to sell your ideas
- Whether you eat breakfast
- How you feel when you come home from work
- What you do when you've made a mistake
- What you do when someone else has made a mistake

- How you react to being stuck in a traffic jam
- What you think about just before you go to sleep at night

Now that you have the idea I'm sure that you could add many choices of your own. None of the items on that list is meant to imply what you should or should not do; that is *always* your choice.

But even that short list does suggest to us how many moments of our days and lives are affected by the choices we make at any given moment.

Look at the opportunities we have to take control and get it right!

What *do* you think about, just before you go to sleep at night? How often in a day or a week or a month *do* you complain about something? How *do* you deal with problems? What *does* make you angry, and *why?* How often *do* you give encouragement to someone else? What *do* you do when you've made a mistake? How often *do* you smile? How polite *are* you? How *do* you feel when you come home from work? Who *do* you talk to when you have a problem?

All of those, and more, are choices. How we handle each of those kinds of choices plays an unbelievably important role in how well we get through each day. They affect how we deal with other people, and a myriad of events in our lives. Many of those choices clearly create how other people treat us.

All of those items may not be on your list of your 100 important choices, but you can be sure that there is a list for you. It isn't even a list that needs to be written down. If you are aware of the choices you make, you'll *know* the next time one comes up! If you did write those choices down on your own list that you could read each day, imagine the advantage that you'd be giving yourself!

Look what you can do, starting anytime you choose, by making conscious, *active* choices every time the opportunity comes up. It is what we do with *these* choices (and many other choices just like them) that will always determine not only how well each day works for us, but how successful we will be at anything we do.

On none of these choices do we really require the help of anyone else. They are all choices we can make for ourselves. Each of them, like the smooth, polished pebbles that join together to form the road that we walk on each day, gives us one more small but solid foundation on which to build our lives.

A woman I met at a seminar I conducted told me she had almost given up trying to make things work for her. "I just feel that I don't have any real say in anything," she told me, "and I don't feel that there's anything I can do to make things better."

No one had ever told her about her choices. No one had ever given her a program that told her, "Your choices are your own, and they are up to you."

Look at the countless number of choices, big and small, that she was not even aware she was making!

We have far greater control over our destinies than we may ever have imagined. As long as we're living life, we can be sure that there will be countless opportunities to make the choices that are presented to us. And we can be sure that those choices will create an important part of what happens next.

"Whatever you choose, you might as well enjoy it.

■

It is your choice."

10

CHOICES OF ATTITUDE

IT MIGHT BE POSSIBLE to go through most of an entire day without ever once consciously thinking about how you "feel" about something—even though any number of things may have happened during that day that created feelings within you.

It might also be possible to go through almost an entire day without ever once consciously thinking about your *behavior*, the actions you're taking. You are simply responding to what's going on around you and within yourself in a very normal and everyday way.

When that happens, your brain doesn't slow down or wait for you to tell it what to do next. It simply moves ahead at high speed and reacts to every neurological nudge and circumstance that is handed to it by sorting through its countless files, determining the appropriate action or response, taking the action, creating the feeling, inspiring the thought, or handling the situation—and your brain does all that without your even being aware of it.

So it isn't that we *need* to tell our own brain what to do every moment—it handles most of its job quite nicely by itself without any conscious input from us at all. But that is also why things often don't go as we would like them to.

Your Brain—the Ultimate Automatic Pilot

It is as though we are putting the airplane on automatic pilot, walking back to the passenger section of our own airplane, and settling down for a nice relaxing nap. When you do that, you can only hope that the programs controlling the computer which drives the automatic pilot are the *right* programs.

Unfortunately, more often than not, the "automatic" programs are not the right programs at all.

Choices of Attitude

If you review the list of 100 choices in the previous chapter, you will notice that each of the choices listed will fit into one of two categories of choices: Choices of Attitude, or Choices of Action.

There are many other subcategories of choices, of course. These have to do with beliefs, emotions, the importance of each choice, etc. But our purpose here is to simplify the process of making choices and, in an easy and natural way, recognize each of the choices that you *can* do something about, and offer some tools that will help.

Choices of Attitude have to do with how you feel about something. This is the kind of feeling that deals with "perspective"—how you look at things. How you see things in life—how you feel about them—is a matter of choice.

It is true that your attitudes are created by your beliefs, and your beliefs are created by your programming. But that doesn't alter the fact that *you can override that programming with new choices that you make on your own, right now*. So how you feel about anything is always your choice.

Four Questions About Your Attitude

There are four questions you can ask yourself in any situation to *immediately* regain conscious control over your attitude—the way you choose to feel about the situation.

Let's say, as an example, that you have been anticipating receiving a raise at work. On Friday morning at 9 o'clock, you are scheduled to have a meeting with your boss or your supervisor, and during that review meeting you will learn whether or not the raise went through.

On Friday morning, you attend the meeting and sit anxiously awaiting the news. Moments later, you are told that a raise will be forthcoming, but that it will be another three months before you receive it.

If that happened to you, how would you feel? Of course, it would depend on a lot of things—your level of expectation, how badly you needed the raise, how you felt about the company you worked for, how good you were at accepting disappointment, and a host of other factors. But at that moment, when that happens, what *really* determines how you feel?

Your feelings at any given moment are always determined or influenced by how you choose to feel at any given moment.

1. How do I feel about this?

Asking yourself this question is the first step in gaining conscious control of your attitude—how you feel. Then give yourself a simple answer—if there is one—and consider it for a moment. How do you feel? Good? Bad? Okay? Happy? Unhappy? Excited? Angry? Nothing at all? Surprised? Relieved?

2. How would I like to feel about this?

Next, ask yourself the second question. More positive? Indifferent? Understanding? Optimistic? Give yourself a clear picture of the feeling you would like to create, if you could.

3. How do I *choose* to feel about this?

How you would *like* to feel about something and how you *choose* to feel about it are two different things. One is a "want"—the other is a choice.

Try this for yourself and watch what happens. Ask yourself those first three questions. And when you reach the question, "How do I choose to feel about this?" give yourself a *specific direction of choice* that says, "I choose to feel '_____' about this," and fill in the blank.

4. How do I feel about this now?

Finally, ask yourself the fourth question: "How do I feel about this *now?*" Chances are, with even a little practice, you'll find that you can, *at almost any time,* change how you feel about almost *anything* by making the choice to change how you feel.

The more often you do this, and the more practice you get, the better it will work for you.

What Having a Good Attitude Really Means

Choices of Attitude do not deal only with how we feel about something like being given bad news, of course. How we feel about *anything* is a Choice of Attitude.

How do you feel about your looks? What are the feelings you have about the weather today? The car you drive? How old you are? How much money you have or do not have in the bank? What you're going to do next weekend? The person you last talked to on the telephone?

When we meet someone who seems to have a "good attitude" about everything, that really isn't the case. That person simply has made a lot of independent choices to have a good attitude about many individual things. Individual choices to view things in a positive and worthwhile way add together to create the personality trait that tells us that individual has a "good attitude."

That personality that we call our "attitude" is nothing more (and nothing less) than the sum total of all the small, daily choices we make—or fail to make—about how we feel.

Give Yourself the Benefit of Choosing Your Own Attitudes

Once you learn that the brain will form your attitudes for you based either on the old programs you received or on the new choices you make, it makes good sense to *tell* your brain how *you* choose to feel now, at any time, at any moment, about anything.

If you understand this process, you will be able to see why past attitudes that may have gotten in your way for years can be stopped and replaced by your choices now. Even if your old programs of the past are deep and strong, you have the ability within you right now to override those old programs of attitude with clear, conscious, determined choices—new programs to your mind.

We have all seen this happen. If you've never been to Paris and have always told yourself that you didn't think you'd like it, and you would not like to go there, what do you think would happen if you were to suddenly win a contest prize of an all-expense-paid trip to Paris?

I remember a friend of mine who decidedly disliked red convertibles until he met and started to date a young lady who drove one. And have you ever known someone who disliked a certain kind of food, but then unwittingly liked it when it was "disguised" as something else?

Situations Are Neutral; Your Attitude Isn't

It is interesting to listen to the form of "Self-Talk" that people use when they talk about what they like or do not like. This Self-Talk, too, is a form of "choices."

These are the kinds of Self-Talk statements that literally *describe to ourselves* how we feel about things— how we look at life, detail by detail. And they are Self-Talk choices that we make *and program ourselves with* day after day, without any regard for the effect that the programs are having in our lives.

Here are just a few examples of situations that people typically react to with either "positive" or "negative" attitudes. How you *feel* about each of the examples on this list is a *Choice of Attitude:*

- Standing in line
- Visiting a certain relative
- Having the same thing for breakfast every morning
- Listening to others without stating your own opinion
- Drinking a cup of coffee
- Answering the telephone
- Being asked to volunteer
- Writing a letter
- Opening the mail
- Fixing dinner
- Helping a child with his schoolwork
- Flying on an airplane
- What you have to wear
- Running an errand
- Having an evening with nothing to do
- Going to a party
- Driving in bad weather
- Watching the news
- Listening to someone with a problem
- Having something break when you need to use it
- Disagreeing with someone
- Dropping something
- Running out of hot water
- Hearing some gossip
- Spilling coffee on your suit
- How bright or how dark the lighting in a room is
- Being told something that isn't true
- The color of the wallpaper
- Having to write a report
- Filling out an expense account
- Doing chores around the house
- Having to meet a schedule or a deadline
- Shopping
- Getting a haircut
- Getting ready in the morning

- Having a family discussion
- Disciplining children
- Receiving a compliment
- Going somewhere in a group
- Eating
- Going out
- Being in a crowd
- Being alone
- Hearing a baby cry
- Moving
- Changing a schedule at the last minute
- Catching a cold
- Making a mistake
- Having someone yell at you
- Waking up in the morning

Some of the situations that are included in this list are similar to those that we looked at earlier in our list of 100 choices. All of them are normal, everyday *situations of the moment* that can typically happen to any of us. How we decide to *feel* about each of them determines how we *react* to them—and what Choices of **Action** we will make next.

*"When you have a problem,
make a choice . . .
you'll feel better."*

11

CHOICES OF ACTION

IN THE PREVIOUS CHAPTER, we discussed that much of how we feel about things—our attitude—is either based on the programs we have received about them in the past, or the choice we have to think about them differently in the present. That means we can change feelings and change or override programs by our choice. The same is also true about "*Choices of Action.*"

These two kinds of choices work hand in hand. Our actions affect our attitudes, and our attitudes affect our actions.

Choices of Action are those choices that tell us not how we feel about something, but what we will do about it. Moment by moment, day after day, we are given the opportunity to make choices about our actions. These are not major decisions about major actions. They can be among the *smallest* decisions that we make. They, too, are important.

Choices of Action include such minor decisions as what to wear, who to talk to, what to say, how to react when someone says something to you, what to eat, what time you'll get up in the morning, which letters to answer and what to write, which street to take on the way to work, whether or not to stop at the store, when to pay the bills, what program you will watch on television, when and if to mow the lawn, what to buy, who to be nice to, which friendships to nurture, where you decide to go on vacation, how to spend five extra minutes of free time, or what time you go to bed at night.

Just as we have the freedom of choice to decide how we feel about anything that comes our way, we also have the freedom of choice to decide what we will *do*—what step we will take or move we will make—in any situation at any time.

Having freedom of choice does not imply that we do not have responsibilities that have to be met, of course. We have jobs, families, homes, social activities, personal relationships, and daily demands of living that, to some extent, seem to dictate many of our choices for us. But it is true that what we decide to do in each instance is still up to us.

If you were to examine the lives of those individuals who are *most* in control of their lives, and compare their Choices of Action with the lives of people who are not achieving success and self-fulfillment, you will always find that those who achieve the best in life exercise more control over the Choices of Action in every detail of their lives.

This is because those who "achieve" take more *personal responsibility* for their own choices. Any of us could do the same. Taking personal responsibility is a habit—*learning to make choices about our actions is a habit*. It is a skill that we learn and develop. If we want to get better at it, we can.

Four Questions About Your Actions

In the previous chapter we asked ourselves four questions about how we felt about our individual perceptions and how we could choose to change the way we felt about each of them if we wanted to.

There are four similar questions that will help you

take control of each of the choices you make that govern your *actions*. They are:

1. What am I doing about this?
2. What would I like to do about this?
3. What do I *choose* to do about this?
4. What am I going to do about this now?

Asking yourself these four questions each time the opportunity comes up can be a fun exercise. Learning to ask these questions naturally and almost automatically could well make the difference in actually doing what you want to do, and in what you will ultimately get out of life.

Taking the few moments to ask yourself these four questions for even a few days or weeks will very clearly show you the importance of the role *you* play in making your "Choices of Action" for yourself.

1. What am I doing about this?

This question asks you to *ask yourself* what to do about the situation—the moment the situation occurs. It could be asked when you are meeting someone for the first time, when you are writing a business report, or when you are talking to one of your children.

Because it is possible to do most of what we do in any given day without giving the matter too much thought, this question *really* asks us the question: "What am I programmed to do in this situation?" What would I usually do? How would I typically act? What action would I usually take, if I did not *think* about my next action *and choose it for myself*?

2. What would I *like* to do about this?

If you could wave your wand, what would you really *like* to do? If you had your way and could do anything you wanted to do at this moment, what would it be?

And this question also asks: "What should I do right now if I want to take the most effective, correct, worthwhile action that I can take?"

All too often, we feel that we are subject to the whims of the world around us. We feel that we "have to" act in a certain way, or that we are "supposed to" do something, or that we are "expected to" do what others want us to do.

Doing any of these—following the expectation— might be completely different than the action we would take if, at the moment, we thought about it and chose for ourselves what we would really like to do.

3. What do I *choose* to do about this?

This question tells you: "What I do next is up to me." Making the choice for yourself puts taking personal responsibility back on you. It accepts your natural birthright for making choices for yourself.

When you ask yourself this question, you put yourself on the line. What you're actually saying is: "This is up to me. *I'm* making the choice. I choose to take personal responsibility for myself, and that's what I'm doing."

4. What am I going to do about this now?

Once you have made the decision to make a choice and act on it, you should find yourself taking action on your choice. That won't always be the case, of course; old programs die hard. There will be times when you will tell yourself that you choose to do one thing, and then find that your old programming convinces you to do another.

It can take time to get used to the fact that a strongly stated personal choice is a powerful new program in itself. Old habits don't let go easily, and old programs love to step back in and regain control.

A new choice made now to not argue at the dinner table, as an example, may be overridden by an old style that makes it all too easy to once again argue when the situation comes up. But the more you choose, the more you direct yourself with your own new choices of change, and the more it will begin to work for you.

You may choose to get up in the morning tomorrow feeling better about yourself and choosing to do those things tomorrow that you know within you will make your day a better day. Some of the new choices will be easier than others, and will work for you the first time you try them. Other choices will take longer.

But if you have not already done so, make the decision to start. Ask yourself, "What am I doing about this? What would I like to do about this? What do I *choose* to do about this? And then watch your response.

"If you'd like to know what your choices have been, look at yourself and the life you have lived.

■

What you see is the choices you've made."

12

THE PATTERN
OF YOUR SUCCESS

THERE ARE THREE PATTERNS or "cycles" that we set up either consciously or unconsciously that control most of how we feel and what we do each day. You will probably find yourself fitting into one of these three patterns.

Understanding these three patterns will help you determine what kind of moment-by-moment choices you have been making in the past, and what choices you would like to make in the future, so that you can decide for yourself which pattern you would like to create and follow in your life. The three patterns are:

1. Pattern I—Choices that build you up.
2. Pattern II—Choices that pull you down.
3. Pattern III—Choices that help you break even.

As we have learned, all of us make choices—either consciously or unconsciously—moment by moment, each day. Each of us makes some choices that build us up, some choices that pull us down, and some choices that help us break even.

But all of us fit generally into one of these three patterns of choices—that is, we tend to make more of our choices in one of the three patterns. If you look closely at the choices you make (especially the smallest choices), you will find that you will fit generally into Pattern I, Pattern II, or Pattern III.

As small or as unimportant as each of those simple choices may appear to be, when added together those choices create the pattern. In time, the pattern of choices that we make creates a cycle, and that cycle forms the shape of a larger pattern that defines for each of us, whether we are aware of it or not, how we live our lives.

Knowing the pattern that you fit into now is important. Knowing the pattern that you'd like to fit into and then making the choices to do something about it is important.

Pattern I People—Choices That Build You Up

People that fit this pattern make even the smallest choices that help them move forward, do better for that moment, create a better day that day, and set themselves up to succeed or to do well.

Instead of saying, "Things just aren't going right for me," when the movie they wanted to see isn't playing, the Pattern I person says, "That's okay. That's fine. We can see something else." When the service in the restaurant isn't up to par, instead of saying, "The service here is terrible," the Pattern I person almost automatically says, "It's really good to have the chance to get out and to relax. The food is great!"

It's not that the Pattern I person sees everything as "perfect" or "wonderful." But the Pattern I person recognizes that life itself isn't always perfect. Things aren't always as he or she would like them to be. *Life exists!* That's how it is.

Recognizing that fact, the Pattern I person uses every opportunity in a productive way—a way to build—a way to get better, instead of seeing life as an obstacle course that only a few can overcome.

It is true that in the category of Pattern I people,

there are the "positive thinkers." But there are also the true achievers, those who take absolute and complete responsibility for themselves, and those who recognize that it is the day-to-day small choices they make about how they feel and what they do that eventually leads them toward their successes in life.

Pattern I people seldom, if ever, complain. They know better. Instead of complaining, they take each situation, see it as it really is, and they make the best of it.

Instead of getting "down" or just "getting by," they choose to see life as a series of opportunities that help them to build and grow.

Your Choices Create the Pattern of Your Life

One small choice leads to another. In each choice you have the opportunity to look at the circumstance in a productive way or in a way that works against you. Good choices lead to more good choices. One good choice sets us up to make another good choice.

In time, these choices link together and begin to form a pattern. The more you make small choices that work for you, the more you will tend to make more choices of the same worthwhile kind. And so the pattern develops.

Let's say that beginning tomorrow morning you decide to spend just one day making choices that always build you up—that work for you instead of against you. Each choice that builds you up makes it easier for you to make another choice that builds you up.

If you do that, even for just one day, it is likely that by tomorrow night, not only will you have made some pretty good choices, but you will feel better about yourself. When we do things that work *for* us, we feel better about ourselves. We add to our self-esteem, and we start to get the feeling that maybe we have more control over our own choices than we might have thought in the past.

What if you decided that beginning tomorrow, even

for just one day, you would do that? What if you did the same thing the next day, and the next? What if you did nothing more than practice always making choices that build you up, even for just one week, and then for a month? Can you imagine what might happen with your attitude—with your *life*—if you made those same Pattern I "build yourself up" choices for a year?

The way you make choices is a habit. Pattern I people are those people who get into the habit of always making choices (especially the small choices) that build them up.

Pattern II People—Choices That Pull You Down

Pattern II people make small choices that pull them down or work against them. They tend to complain instead of making the best of a difficult situation, they see the risk instead of the opportunity, or they have the habit (a pattern of choices) of looking at the worst first and the best last.

Pattern II people create the rain that falls on their own parade. They see life as an endless series of struggles instead of always seeing the exact same situations as an endless series of challenges and chances to grow or feel good about themselves.

Pattern II people tend to be negative Self-Talkers. Without even thinking about it, they tend to say things like: "I just know this won't work"; "I'm already late for work and I can't believe it—another red light"; "Why even open the mail? All I ever get is bills"; "Every time I talk to him we have an argument"; "Today just isn't my day"; "We never get good service at this restaurant"; "I could never be that lucky"; or "I never have anything to wear."

All of these statements and countless others like them are choices, of course. If you want to know who the Pattern II people around you are, listen to their Self-Talk—listen to their choices.

While Pattern I people have learned that complaining

is usually an unnecessary choice—a choice that works against you—Pattern II people complain more, and they usually do it without even thinking about it, without ever recognizing that it is their choice.

Pattern II people see the dark instead of the dawn. They tell you what won't work instead of what will. Pattern II people aren't always unhappy, of course. They are normal, everyday people who make small choices that pull them down instead of building them up. And without ever knowing what they are doing, they create a descending cycle of choices that lead them downward into a self-made canyon from which they can no longer see the horizon.

It is as though they are building a path, stone by stone, choice by choice, that takes them down instead of up. They are compelled to continue a journey of despair without ever recognizing that they alone are laying the stones that form the pathway. It is not a happy path. But it is one that is built by the littlest of choices—choices that could have, instead, with the exact same amount of energy and effort, built a roadway that would have led them toward happiness and success.

Not all Pattern II people live in despair, of course. There are degrees of unhappiness. Some Pattern II people fare better in life than others. But for the most part, Pattern II people pull themselves down instead of building themselves up.

Pattern III People—Choices That Keep You Breaking Even

The largest group of people is the group that fits into Pattern III. These are the people who make choices that help them break even, but get them nowhere. They do okay. They survive. Because of the choices they make, they never really get anywhere or reach a level of self-fulfillment that approaches achieving their true potential. But on the other hand, they never get too far down either. They break even.

The reason that most of the people you or I will ever

meet fall into this category is because the choices in this pattern are always the easiest and most automatic. Most of the Pattern III people seldom recognize that there is any real choice to make at all.

The primary program of the people who live in Pattern III is the program of going along with the crowd, staying in line, and fitting in. There is certainly nothing wrong with being a Pattern III person—but there is also nothing very right about it.

Psychologists tell us that it is the Pattern III person who is quietly frustrated with life, but isn't sure why. It is in this pattern that we drift through life instead of making the choice to set a clearly defined direction. We worry about "keeping up with the Joneses" when, in fact, we *are* the Joneses.

Pattern III people avoid making choices that create waves or upset the norm. They survive and they get along, but for the most part, they simply exist. They do everything they are "supposed to" do. And they never come close to reaching a fraction of the potential they could have achieved in their lives.

In discussing people who make "get by" choices and live their lives in Pattern III, I am not suggesting that they should do otherwise. Those individuals in Pattern III usually live lives that are good and worthwhile. They may not build monuments to their successes, but they do get through life in a reasonably fulfilling way.

Choice by choice, day by day, they ensure themselves of breaking even. Instead of being recognized as Pattern I people of notable achievement, or Pattern II people of self-created defeat, Pattern III people quietly fall into being a statistic in the status quo.

If that is their choice, no one should suggest they do otherwise. But, I often wonder how many Pattern III people might make their choices a little differently if they had learned they could utilize a great deal more of the potential they were born with if only they had not bought into the habit of making choices that took them out of the running.

The Choices You Make Create the Pattern of Who You Are

Think of three people that you know well. Get a good picture of each of them in your mind. Now ask yourself the question about each of them: "Is this person a Pattern I person, a Pattern II person, or a Pattern III person?" If you think about it, even for a few moments, you should be able to determine in which of the three patterns each of the friends you have chosen fits best. And after you have a clear picture in your mind where each of them fits, ask yourself a second question about each of them: "How 'successful' is this person?" And then ask a third question: "How happy or fulfilled is this person?"

If you were to write on the top of three separate pieces of paper the words, "Pattern I People I Know," "Pattern II People I Know," and "Pattern III People I Know," and then list on those three sheets of paper people you now know or have known in the past, and then asked yourself the same three questions about each of them, what do you suppose you would find?

I suspect you would find that the people you listed on the sheet of paper titled "Pattern I People I Know" would be the happiest and most successful. Those listed on the sheet entitled "Pattern II People I Know" would be the people you have known who are the least happy and in many ways the least successful people. The people you listed on the sheet entitled "Pattern III People I Know" would probably be generally happy or "okay."

Now ask yourself why some of them were happy and fulfilled, some of them were unhappy and unfulfilled, and some of them were in between. If you recognized that it was the choices they made along the way—especially the smallest choices that created their patterns—that made them who they are today, give yourself a gold star. You have figured out one of the most important keys to human behavior and the achievement of potential that any of us can ever learn.

"Who knows what you could accomplish in life if you made more of the right choices along the way?"

13

10 STEPS TO BECOMING A PATTERN I PERSON

I F YOU WOULD LIKE the simplest of your everyday choices to guide you toward success instead of away from it, there are 10 simple steps you can follow that will help. You don't have to memorize these steps, but you should become familiar with them.

If becoming a Pattern I person is important to you, or if you are already a Pattern I person and would like to do it better, you might like to make a photocopy of these few pages that list the steps, and for the next week or so carry them with you and reread them from time to time. It would be worth the effort.

If we knew each other personally and you were to ask me what you could do, right now, to put into effect the most positive and worthwhile choices in your life, I would suggest to you that you follow these 10 steps. In time, and with a little practice, the steps would become automatic. You wouldn't have to think about them at all.

If you follow the steps carefully for even a few days or a week or two, you will have the solution for yourself. No matter what choices you may have been making in the past, you will begin to become a Pattern I person.

10 Steps to Becoming a Pattern I Person

1. Decide what pattern you are now.

Be honest about this. Does the sum of the little choices you make, day in and day out, build you up, pull you down, or help you break even? It is important here to recognize that it doesn't make any difference what your choices have been in the past, and what patterns you may have created for yourself until now. If you want to change your pattern, you can.

You should also know that if you make the decision to change your choices, you will in time begin to change the fundamental programs that will direct the choices you will make in the future. That's good news! None of us has to live with the old programs we have received in the past that may have worked against us. Once you recognize where you have been or where you are now, and make the decision for yourself that you want to do something about it—you can!

2. Ask yourself, "Is my present program working for me or isn't it?"

You already know whether your current pattern of choices is working for you or if it isn't. The key here is to *tell* yourself whether it is or not.

3. Carefully look at the patterns of choices of the people around you.

As we have already seen, taking a careful look at the patterns of choices that other people around us have been using tells us a great deal about what works and what doesn't. Make a conscious effort to look at the styles of choices that other people are using.

(When you do this, don't make the mistake of telling them that they might be doing something wrong. They certainly don't want your advice, and unless they understand patterns of choices, there is a good chance they wouldn't understand what you're talking about anyway.)

Just learn to observe. And remember, it's the "little" choices you're looking for. If you watch carefully, it should not take long for you to notice the direct connection between "good small choices" and people who are working at self-fulfillment.

4. Make a list of the choices that would improve your pattern.

This one takes a little time, but it's worth it. What are the choices you could write down that would help you become a Pattern I person? The choices you write down could be almost anything. Remember, we're talking here about "little" choices—how you dress, how you listen, what you say, the way you talk, who you spend time with, what you do after work or in the evening— almost anything at all.

Keep your list of new Pattern I choices short—no more than ten items on the list. Then write them down on a pocket card, carry them with you, and read through your list a few times each day for the next week.

I wish I could tell you how important this small suggestion is. This one simple step could do more for recognizing and adjusting the rest of the choices you make than anything else.

5. Learn to recognize the old programs that could be holding you back.

This one isn't so easy. It is sometimes difficult to figure out the programs we carry in our minds that are stopping us or holding us back. If you'd like some help on this one, go back and reread Chapter 2, "Who Are You and What Do You Want?". Every program you have came from somewhere. Learning to recognize where those old programs came from and what role they still play in our lives today will tell you a lot about why you have continued to make the choices you have been making.

Remember that understanding who you are and what you really want out of life—once you start thinking about it—plays an incredibly important role in the choices that you will make next.

6. Decide which programs you want to work on most.

If you uncover an old program that you would like to change, go to work on it. What you think today, what you want today, counts far more than the programs you may have been given in the past. Old programs from the past hold us back because we let them.

Few of our old programs that work against us go away by accident. They have to be replaced or overridden. Maybe it's time to clean house. Decide which programs you want to work on most. Throw out the old ideas and notions and beliefs that have been holding you back. Dust off, fix up and display the programs you want to keep.

Can you really do that? Yes, you can! Some of the right Self-Talk will help, but deciding for yourself which of your programs you really want to hold on to, to play a role in the life that you're living now, is an excellent first step.

7. Beginning immediately, start practicing Pattern I choices.

Beginning tomorrow morning, start making choices that build you up. Starting with the moment you awake, there is the opportunity to see things differently, to respond to every situation in the most positive, productive, and worthwhile way. Just imagine what a day you have in store for you!

From the time you get out of bed to the time you go to sleep tomorrow night, you will probably have a few dozen or a few hundred opportunities to make choices. Use them well. Recognize that every moment of the day is an opportunity to make choices that build you up, pull you down, or get you to break even.

8. Assess your progress—watch the feedback you get from yourself and from others.

When you become aware of the many choices that are yours to make—even in just one day—and when you make those choices for yourself, you will start to see yourself differently. So will others around you. Some of them may like it, and some of them may not. But keep your own counsel.

Remember, you are living your life, not theirs. You have the right to make your choices for yourself—they don't. (They should be busy enough taking responsibility for their own choices.)

When you begin to take responsibility for making your own choices, some of those you make will cause you to feel differently about yourself. Some of what you feel may be uncomfortable. Most of it will feel good. But don't worry about feeling ill at ease; that just means it's working. Change often produces anxiety. But when you feel good about even the smallest choice you have made because *you* chose to make it—enjoy it!

9. Set a clear, solid goal to become a Pattern I person.

Pattern I people create a pattern of success throughout their lives by making the smallest choices that work for them. If you want to do it, do it! If you don't want to make little choices that work for you, that is okay. Only you can determine what you really want to get out of the life you are living.

Here is a test. Right now, stop for a moment and ask yourself these three questions:

- Do I want to make choices that build me up?
- Do I want to make choices that hold me back?
- Do I want to make choices that do nothing more than help me break even?

Your answers to those three questions, if you think about it, will be without a doubt one of the most important decisions you will ever make.

10. Reward yourself along the way.

Once you begin the process of forming and shaping even the smallest of your choices in a way that always builds you up, you will soon recognize that making good choices takes some effort. In time, it will become automatic, natural, a way of life; but to begin with, it takes some work.

To help you keep going, it is essential that you give yourself some rewards along the way. Whether you give yourself a gift, a night out three weeks in a row, or simply an acknowledgment from you to yourself, make a point of recognizing what you are accomplishing. Recognize that it was begun by you in the first place, and that it is you who are making it happen. Give credit where credit is due. That is part of taking responsibility for yourself.

Reward yourself. Talk to yourself. Tell yourself every day that you are doing this for yourself and that you are achieving your goal. From the moment you become one of the few who take the personal responsibility of making choices that build, and never again make a single choice that could possibly hold you back or do nothing more than let you break even in life, you will at the same time create some exceptional rewards in your life. When you make choices for yourself, life changes for the better.

But meanwhile, let yourself know you're doing okay. After all, you are doing something that few people ever do. You are, by yourself, taking control of the rest of your life.

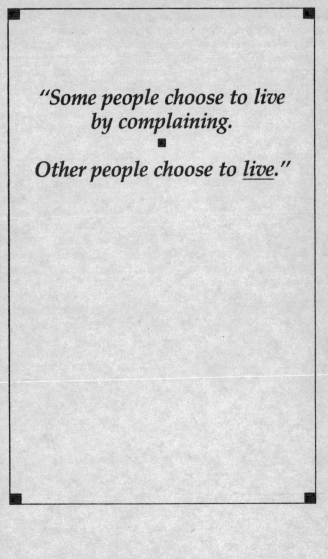

"Some people choose to live by complaining.

■

Other people choose to <u>live</u>."

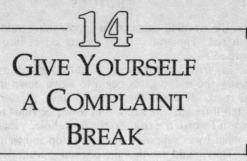

14

GIVE YOURSELF
A COMPLAINT
BREAK

NOT ONLY IS IT TRUE that we create many of our own problems for ourselves, but it is also true that we make things worse by what we think and what we say when the problem occurs. Until we know better, all of us complain from time to time. Some people complain more than others, and we have all known those who live their lives by complaining and never really live at all. And yet, complaining, too, is a choice. None of us really have to do it. It is just one of those seemingly "harmless" habits that we picked up along the way.

Like all of our habits, whether we complain or not is the result of our programming. We know it doesn't really help anything, but we do it anyway. And we may never even stop to realize the effect that the habit of complaining has on our lives.

Making Things Work by Calling on Your Best

A friend of mine was recently driving through crosstown traffic with a companion on the way to a concert, and it was important that they arrive on time. They had left in plenty of time to get there on schedule, but just as they approached one of the few railroad crossings in the city, the warning lights of an approaching train began to flash red. The traffic gates swung down into the stop position.

My friend told me what went through his mind when he saw the traffic gates begin to move down in front of the road. "I knew that I could have accelerated and gotten through," he said, "but it was obvious to me that it wasn't worth the risk. So the first choice I made was to do what I was supposed to do and stop and wait."

They could see that the oncoming train was moving slowly, and was pulling an endless line of railroad cars behind it. It was obvious that their wait would be a long one.

"I sized up the situation and decided to make a second choice. Before either my friend who was riding with me or I could say anything about the fact that the delay would cause us to be late, I turned the ignition off, turned to my friend and said, 'Let's count the cars.' And that's what we did."

In recounting the story to me, my friend told me that he realized the moment he stopped that he could do the obvious—complain about the problem, and possibly let the delay end up ruining the evening for both of them.

"When I was a small boy," he said, "I used to love to count the cars when we had to wait for a train. Instead of allowing myself to get upset, I decided to take myself back and enjoy the part of me that could count train cars without worrying about the pressures and the schedules that grown-ups have. It was great!" he said. "I actually enjoyed the opportunity. And I knew that it was a choice."

The small choice that my friend made in that situation may seem like a very insignificant one. And yet it is so typical of the circumstances that confront each of us in different ways every day.

Instead of allowing himself to become upset and respond in the poorest possible way to a situation he was in—and had no control over at the moment—he simply chose to make a better choice.

I sometimes wonder how many of the stresses many of us feel each day are not so much the result of the situations we face, but rather the result of what we choose to do about them.

I'm not suggesting that we should always think everything is wonderful even when it isn't, or ignore problems that need to be dealt with. There is a time to stand our ground and refuse to accept the inadequacies or the flaws in life that make things difficult for us.

But we're not talking here about the right each of us has to state our piece and to do our best to change something that should be changed, nor about the times we feel compelled to make positive suggestions that clearly serve a worthwhile purpose.

We are talking, instead, about the kind of complaints that we hear every day from so many people around us. This is the kind of complaining that never really seems to help. If anything, it makes us feel worse—never better— and never really accomplishes anything worthwhile at all.

This is the kind of complaining that does nothing more than express dissatisfaction, tell us we are unhappy with something, or give us the opportunity to complain out loud. It is a negative attitude about the way things are.

Little Complaints That Really Aren't

If we really wanted to, I suppose any of us could always find something to complain about. Most of the time, there are plenty of opportunities for any of us to complain about something, if we choose to. Here is a list of just a few things that even well-intentioned individuals can allow, time after time, to undermine their attitudes and upset their day:

- The weather
- Traffic
- Airline delays
- Waiting in line

- Food service in restaurants
- Children
- Things the other political party does
- Most of the things that happen at work
- Things in the news
- Things the neighbors do
- The postal service
- Things that break
- Losing something
- Having to work
- Food prices
- Television
- Road construction
- Medical costs
- Relatives
- Physical ailments that won't go away
- Things in the past
- Not having done something they wanted to do
- The way other people look
- The way other people act
- The music other people listen to
- What time it is
- Taxes
- Being late
- Other people being late
- People not listening to them
- Following rules
- Waiting
- Their paycheck
- The car not starting

I would add to that list a host of inconveniences that may seem trivial, but are often emotionally charged. There are many small, almost unnoticeable occurrences that cause no problem at all for some people; but for others they can unleash a virtual tirade of frustration and complaint.

In spite of the fact that we all know we will live through these and other similar adversities, we sometimes allow them to affect us in a way that is out of proportion to the situation. In the process, we do nothing more than lower our attitude and reinforce negative programs in our minds.

Most complaining has no worthwhile value at all, and few of us recognize the harm that we create within ourselves by doing it.

It's More Than Just Blowing Off Steam

You may have known people who justified their habit of complaining by saying that they were "blowing off steam," "getting it off their chest," or just "stating their mind." When people complain, they may have no idea what they are really doing to themselves. The simple act of stating a complaint, even when it is stated without thinking about it, creates immediate—and often strong—chemical and electrical changes in the brain.

When you complain, you create programs in the mind that work against you instead of for you. If your feelings at the moment are strong enough—if your words are laced with strong emotion—you will automatically set up a natural chemical response in the brain that will affect your thoughts, your attitude, your behavior, your stress level, and even the physiological processes in the brain that control your physical health and well-being.

Until recently, few of us were aware of the profound effect that something as simple as complaining could have on each of us. Complaining seemed like a natural thing to do, almost an ordinary part of everyday life. But the subconscious mind accepts every complaint as a *program*. It prints it, stores it for future reference and use, and responds to it.

That response—whether our complaint was stated openly, thought about, or even stated to ourselves without thinking about it—puts into motion a complex mechanism in the brain that unconsciously and automatically affects us and directs us, not just at the moment that we state the complaint, but often for the minutes or hours that follow. That intricate and complex electrical and chemical response in the brain goes to work to literally affect or control who we are, how we feel, how and what we think, and what we do next.

When you program yourself with the habit of complaint, here is what happens:

- Complaining negatively affects your attitude—immediately, and over a period of time.
- Complaining creates additional negative programming in your brain.
- Complaining creates negative, unhealthy side effects—especially stress.
- Complaining replaces objectivity with frustration, adding unnecessary *emotion* to the situation.
- Complaining makes you quietly or openly angry.
- Complaining attracts others to you who are also negative.
- Complaining makes people like you less.
- Complaining usually doesn't do any good, and it helps you put off making a choice that could solve the problem.
- Complaining creates a picture of life that is not accurate.
- Complaining is contagious—it affects others.
- Complaining forms and reinforces a habit of looking at the negative.
- Complaining causes you to miss seeing the "good" while you dwell on the "bad."
- Complaining reinforces a picture of yourself (your self-esteem) that is injured or inadequate.
- Complaining makes you think, because you do it, that it is "okay" to complain.
- Complaining turns vital, positive or productive mental energy into mental and physical energy that works against you.
- Complaining reinforces childhood attitudes of "not getting your way" instead of building important attitudes of maturity.

- Complaining puts the problem in control and takes the control of the situation away from you.
- Complaining uses up energy that is essential for making your day work well.
- Complaining reduces your effectiveness as an individual.

The items on that list alone should convince anyone that it doesn't make any sense to choose to complain. If you think about it, why would you ever deal with an annoyance or a problem by telling your brain: "Make this problem worse. Make me feel bad about this"? Why would we, consciously or even unconsciously, set ourselves up for a bad moment, a physiologically unhealthy hour, or a mentally "down" day because we chose to complain instead of choosing not to?

When you realize how much control you have over the chemistry of your mind, which affects and directs your own feelings, isn't it astonishing to think that those who recognize what they are doing to themselves by spending a day (or even a few moments out of that day) complaining, might choose to continue to do it?

5,000 Minutes a Year

Now let's consider the impact of not just a few moments or days in which complaints cause your chemicals and attitudes to work against you, but all of the moments and days added together.

Even one minute of complaining can play havoc with our minds. And if an individual who has not yet learned that complaining—or not complaining—is a choice, spent no more than fifteen minutes a day causing himself or herself to complain or be upset about the normal difficulties of the day, those few minutes of self-imposed aggravation would add up to *more than 5,000 irreplaceable minutes* of powerfully negative self-programs in just one year.

And it is not only those thousands of minutes of

complaint or negative feelings that affect us. Those simple moments of complaint create *hours* of supporting attitudes which are just as negative. Many times after the complaint itself is long gone, and perhaps even forgotten, the feeling lingers on—it affects everything else about us.

That is why when one small thing goes wrong, *everything* can go wrong. We have adjusted our attitude to respond in a negative way—not just to the problem that created the attitude in the first place, but to whatever else happens next.

A "Bad Day"—or a Bad Choice?

I know people who have had a "bad day" simply because something went wrong the first thing that morning, and they unknowingly chose to see the problem through the self-imposed filter of anger or complaint. With this choice, they allowed a small problem to destroy their enthusiasm and happiness *for an entire day,* instead of calling up a healthier, more mature response that would have helped them to see the problem as nothing more than what it really was.

I have known people whose entire vacations were ruined by one flat tire. I have known people who allowed a ten-minute argument in the morning to destroy an entire day. I have watched people in airports, as an example, destroy their composure and ruin the entire day ahead over an airline flight that was delayed because the weather was bad.

We have all seen people who have allowed the smallest occurrence to upset an entire day. One woman who attended a seminar I conducted on Self-Talk and self-programming told me that she had spent five years being upset the first hour every morning because she couldn't find the right clothes to wear!

Another man told me that he arrived at work in a bad mood almost every day because of the traffic conditions he faced each day on the way to work. Because he had not yet recognized that complaining—or not complaining—was a choice, he had created months of unnecessary aggravation for himself by allowing himself to be misdirected by a self-imposed "problem" that was probably unavoidable in the first place.

The problem that created the "bad day" for each of these people in the first place may have been something they could do nothing about. But instead of using their own resources to view the problem in a practical and objective way, they chose to complain about it without ever once stopping to recognize that the *real* problem was in how they looked at the problem and themselves in the first place.

You *Can* Choose Not to Complain

The reason it is important to take a close look at complaining is that while the problem creating the complaint in the first place may be unavoidable and out of our control, the attitude itself is a *choice*. We can control our choices; how we feel about the problem and how we *think about it* is always up to each of us.

You—if you choose—can always decide what you complain or feel bad about. In the real world problems come up and we have to deal with them. But *how* you deal with problems—each and every one of them—will always be a choice.

If you are in control of *you*, no one else can make that choice for you. And once you recognize that it *is* your choice, that whether you complain or instead put a smile on your face and move on is entirely in your hands—it really doesn't make any sense at all to keep complaining.

Your Energy Is a Treasure—So Use It Wisely

If, at birth, you were given a small treasure chest that held only a few precious, irreplaceable gems of energy that you could spend and use up in your lifetime, where would you spend them and how would you use those gems? Would you waste your precious energy by spending it on the unnecessary exertion of complaining, or would you use that precious energy on something else?

If you had only a few small, precious gems of time and energy left, would you cast them away by using them to write a small and unimportant story that described the little failings and inconveniences of life, or would you use them instead, if you could, to paint a bright and shining portrait of your potential?

That *is* how it is. Each of us, from the moment of birth, is given a limited amount of energy and time, and the opportunity to do something with them. And what you do with your time, your energy, and every one of your thoughts and words, is entirely up to you.

You make the choice whether or not to complain about, feel bad about or, for even a moment, become upset about any of the moments in life that just don't go your way. It is an exceptionally important choice, but fortunately, an easy choice to make. You will either complain or you won't. But if you truly care about yourself—and I believe that you do—then spend your treasure wisely.

What We Could Gain by Choosing Not to Complain

Imagine the incredibly powerful, productive moments, minutes and hours of the days and weeks of our lives that we could complain or not—simply by our own choices. I doubt that we could accurately calculate the amount of additional productive time each of us would have in one year if, for that year, we turned every moment of complaint into a moment of choice to do something better instead.

Over the years, I have worked with many companies and organizations who were working hard to improve their morale and productivity. I have often wondered what those companies could do and what achievements they could reach if they did nothing more than infuse each of their managers and employees with the simple message that "Attitude is a choice. Complaining destroys; personal responsibility always builds."

Imagine what we could do in our homes, with our families and in our personal lives if we made the choice to replace complaining with positive belief. Imagine what you could do with those extra moments and hours of your life if you made the choice, right now, to never again complain—and at every opportunity from here on out to replace even the most minor complaint with the positive energy of your own potential. *Just imagine what you could do!*

Imagine *never again* complaining. Could you still be a strong person, a person of conviction and opinion? Would you still do everything you need to do to make changes in your life, or to deal in a clear and effective way with the obstacles and problems that come along? The answer is that you would be *more* effective. You would be better than ever as you would be concentrating on positive actions to improve situations.

Those are not the words of some motivational speaker or an inspirational message. They are simply the truth.

Take a Complaint Break

If you would like to be rid, once and for all, of the frustrations and anxieties that problems create in your life or may have created in the past, the solution is simple. Make a choice. It's entirely up to you!

You can let life's little difficulties bother you, or you can choose to look at them as an adult. You can let normal, everyday occurrences affect you in a way that makes things worse, or you can choose not to.

So give yourself a break. Give yourself a break from

spending your important thoughts and energies (that you most certainly need and could use elsewhere in your life) on the unnecessary habit of complaining about anything.

If you want to receive the best from the life you live, you will first have to give it your best. Never give it anything less. That is your choice.

"You cannot manage your life if you do not manage your self.

∎

You cannot manage your self if you do not manage your choices.

∎

Manage your choices, and you will manage your life."

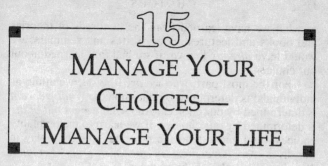

15

MANAGE YOUR CHOICES— MANAGE YOUR LIFE

L ET'S TAKE A MOMENT now and look at what we're discussing from the broad perspective. Let's find out where we've been and where we're going.

From what we have seen so far, the implications of "being aware of our choices" are profound and life-changing. In fact, few of us would argue with the basic message that: The more we are aware of the choices we make, the better the choices we will make; the better our choices, the better off we become.

Having read this far one might wonder why we are not *all* naturally expert in making choices *already*—why we would have to make ourselves more *aware*, or why we would have to *practice* making choices at all. Shouldn't this practice already be a *way of life* for all of us? And yet there are people who spend an entire lifetime without ever getting it right.

Is it possible that the essential importance of understanding *choices* is so obvious that we sometimes miss its importance entirely?

Learning About Choices Takes Us Back to the Basics of What Our Lives Are About

Having studied the field of Personal Development for nearly two decades, I have become convinced that most of what we have learned from the hundreds of theories and books and lectures and cassettes and seminars, we would have *already* known, if we had *first* learned about our choices.

For the most part, *who we are* (the *self* we attain as individuals) is determined by our choices. *What we want* is determined by our choices. And *what we get out of life* is determined by our choices. If we learn to make quality choices—and understand the powerful role they play in our lives—*we have most of the basics of "Personal Development" already figured out*.

So it is surprising that, as adults, we should have to practice a form of "self-management" that should already be an everyday habit—taught to us almost from birth. And yet for many of us it is an awareness and a habit that we are now learning—*really* learning—for the first time.

As humans, we have developed the ability to see life from dozens of perspectives, and yet we somehow ignore something that lies at the very core of us getting through it.

That is hard to believe when, at the same time, we learn so much about life and the world we live in. We see the big picture of life as a personal epic that takes us from birth to old age. And yet we have the incredible ability to spend hours of time focusing on life's most minor details, such as picking out the fabric for the new drapes, or reading pages of minor and forgettable news items in the morning paper.

We also spend hours, days, or even months planning major events in our lives—education, marriages, and careers, for example.

So we clearly have the ability to focus on both the large and the small aspects of our existence. We are obviously aware of the importance of bettering ourselves—and hundreds of personal improvement books, programs, seminars, lectures, and videos attest to the fact that we recognize the improvement of ourselves as a worthwhile pursuit.

With all of that perspective, with all of that awareness, with all of that enthusiasm for making our lives better, it is astounding that so few people are ever taught the basics of doing the one thing that everything else we do hinges upon—making choices.

During the past few years we have made significant leaps forward in our understanding of how the brain works and about why we do what we do. We have learned that all success eventually comes through what we now call Self-Management—that is, taking personal responsibility for the management of our own minds, and thereby taking control over our lives.

In understanding how we act out the strongest programs that are stored electrically and chemically in the brain, we have opened important doors in the understanding of how to manage ourselves more effectively— and in ways that are natural to the normal programming process of the human brain.

Everything we learn about this process invariably leads to the same conclusion: managing your self always begins with managing your choices.

There can be no effective Self-Management without first taking full and complete conscious control over every choice you make.

And yet, even with this knowledge readily available to us, it is still possible to attend lectures or seminars or pick up the latest books on personal improvement and find that they once again show us a glorious picture of our tomorrows, or give us some new method or technique to grow and live better today, without identifying the fact that *unless you learn to manage your choices and the programs those choices create in the subconscious mind, you cannot effect permanent change.*

In time, schools will likely teach "Choice-Management" as a regular part of a standard curriculum. Our children, or their children, will one day be taught the basics of Self-Management. They will be taught about the brain and programming, the skill of making choices, and the important basic personal skill of *managing* their thinking and themselves.

Today, or tomorrow, when you are driving in traffic, standing on a street corner, or walking through a shopping mall, look around you and ask yourself the question, "How many of the people around me are truly conscious, active Self-Managers? How many of them are managing their thoughts, their programming, and their choices each and every day?"

I doubt that we could find a single one of those people who does not truly want to achieve the best for herself or himself in life. We would probably find that many of them are doing something about it; they're working hard to better themselves in every way they can.

We would also find that many of them, even the most positive among them, are often frustrated by the roadblocks and pitfalls that their own past programming creates for them.

And we would probably find that many of them, though they have the best intentions and they're headed in the right direction, have never become aware that one of the most important solutions they could ever hope to use to help them get where they are going is as close as the next choice they make.

In fact, one of the most remarkable aspects of Choice-Management is that anyone who *thinks* can do it. You can begin doing it immediately, there is nothing difficult about it, and it quickly becomes a habit.

I feel for those who work so hard at becoming good Self-Managers and who wonder what's going wrong when it is almost as though they missed the first day of class— the day the teacher talked about the bedrock, the basis of all Self-Management—*conscious choices*.

Could it be that success in Self-Management could be that simple? We certainly have enough methods and ideas and advice on how to handle the *rest* of our Self-Management. Could it be that if we added this one simple process of *making choices,* that the other techniques and methods we have learned would work better—in fact, actually succeed?

Yes, it could.

If you are currently working in any way to better yourself, fix a problem, reach a goal, or conquer a challenge, and are not using Choice-Management with every opportunity that comes along, I encourage you to do so. If you do, I suspect you may be in for some exciting and delightful surprises.

its half... as I have learned would save you half—pay—pay—
supply and cost.

If you are already over the grind and to being
you are set to trade, the fresh to read the chance a case
if you and the old things know M. Manhattan with even
time during the chance using 1. chance a chance to read
sell. Also, I suggest you may be in for some reading and
the same.

"Learning <u>what</u> to choose, and <u>how</u> to choose, may be the most important education you will ever receive."

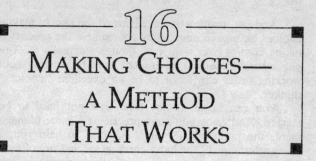

16

MAKING CHOICES—
A METHOD
THAT WORKS

IT HAS BEEN SAID that "thinking is not easy," and that
is perhaps why so few people ever engage in it. But the
kind of thinking that helps us understand who we are and
what we want, what's going on, and what choices we
really want to make—that kind of thinking is *not* difficult.

How many of us were ever actually taught in school
how this process of thinking and choosing actually
works? We sat through classes in reason and logic,
learned what critical thinking skills are all about, and
even learned some things about right-brain thinking and
creativity.

But for most of us, no one ever sat us down and told
us: "This is how it works. This is how Choice-Management operates. This is how you practice it."

And unfortunately, because a "style" of thinking
becomes an electrically and chemically imprinted *pattern*
of thinking in the brain, once our basic thinking style was
in place, few of us questioned how we thought, what we
thought, how the process works, or what we were missing
out on by not understanding it.

Look at the amount of potential control over our
own choices we have and therefore the control we have
over much of what happens *to* us.

And yet, many who have learned the skill of making choices have been amazed by how simple the process of taking control over their own thoughts actually is. *Anyone* whose biological equipment is in reasonably good working order can learn to be an excellent "choices" thinker.

You can begin at any time. It's not hard to get started. And once you start practicing Choice-Management, the brain takes over and begins to help you. It takes advantage of the habit-creating mechanism of mental programs and starts to get you actively managing your thinking and your choices naturally and automatically.

Effective Techniques for Managing Your Choices

There are several methods and techniques that I recommend for becoming a top-notch Choice-Manager. The first method is a simple, four-step thought process that you can apply at any time. It's easy to use, and it is an effective way to help yourself become more aware of your choices as they come up throughout each day. It also helps you make good choices.

The next time even the possibility of a choice comes up, follow these four simple steps:

The Four Steps of Choice

1. Say to yourself (or out loud, if you want to), *"Is this a choice?"*

2. If the answer is yes, then immediately say to yourself, *"This choice is mine."*

3. Next, as soon as you have given the choice as much or as little thought as it requires, consciously say or think to yourself the words, *"My choice is . . ."* and complete the sentence.

4. Always be *aware* at a conscious level of why you have made the choice. Say to yourself, *"The*

reason I made this choice is . . .'' This is to keep
you fully on top of which of your mental programs
you are responding to, and who or what is in
control of your decisions.

You might like to write those four steps down on an
index card and carry the card around with you for a few
days. The steps are simple enough, and easy to follow,
but it sometimes helps to have an instant, word-for-word
visual reminder written down.

This simple method will work for any choice at any
level. You should do it often enough so that it becomes a
habit. You go through the steps quickly, ask the question,
make the assessment and come to a conscious choice so
normally that instead of it seeming like a chore (having
to *think*), it becomes a natural way of thinking.

People who get into the habit of practicing thought-
starter techniques such as this seem to surprise themselves at how natural and easy it is after they have been
doing it for a while. But before you get started, it can
sound like a real chore. Fortunately, because of the way
the brain works, it's not a chore at all.

In actual practice, *any new style of thinking, once it
becomes a habit, does not require extra effort, and in
time becomes a natural way of thinking*.

The next time you're on your way home from work
and the thought pops into your head that you may need
to put gas in the car, ask yourself the question, *''Is this a
choice?''* (It is.) Say the words to yourself, *''This is my
choice,''* and then say the words, *''My choice is . . .* (to
stop for gas, or not to stop),'' and sum it up by telling
yourself *why*.

That entire process takes only a few moments. If
practiced even in that one circumstance, the process
would certainly create some positive benefits for anyone
who rides on ''empty'' or gets to work late because he
has to stop for gas in the morning.

That's a simple example, but it illustrates how naturally and easily the technique can be used—and with some very beneficial results.

Let's use another example. Let's say you are working late, the job you're finishing may take longer than you expected, and there's a good chance you're going to get home late and someone might worry.

The thought of calling home crosses your mind. In the past you may have dodged the thought, put it off, or made a half-hearted decision that made your mental programs take over and make the decision for you. The result was that you didn't call home, someone worried, and a spat took place that could easily have been avoided.

So this time, because you are a "Choices-Thinker," the moment the thought of calling home comes to your mind, you *automatically* ask yourself the question: *"Is this a choice?"* (Yes, it is.) Make the simple statement to yourself, *"This is my choice."* Then say, *"My choice is . . ."* completing the statement yourself. Then tell yourself *why,* and take whatever action you choose. (I'd call home.)

Or how about a bigger choice? You have friends visiting from out of town for a long weekend, and by the time Sunday evening comes, your friends implore you to take Monday off to spend more time together.

You'd like to take the time, and you don't want to disappoint your friends, but you also have commitments at work.

You ask yourself the question, *"Is this a choice?"* (Yes, it is). You say to yourself the words, *"This is my choice."* And then, after the appropriate thought, you say, *"My choice is . . ."* and you state your choice clearly and strongly to yourself. You complete the process by telling yourself *why.*

Let's say that in this instance your decision is to go to work. By going through these few simple steps, your choice becomes clearer to you, you are sure that it is your choice and not someone else's, and you clearly understand the reasons for the action you are taking.

Not only does that process help you make the choice

(and more frequently the right choice), but it also helps you accept the *responsibility* for the results of the decision you made.

When we do not clearly take responsibility for the choice being ours in the first place, we often have trouble accepting the *results* of the choice that we made.

Results are always easier to accept when we take personal responsibility for creating them. And when we take the personal responsibility for making that choice in the first place, our chances of creating *better* results are always greater.

Using this four-step technique for making choices also helps clear up another common problem—the habit of making a decision and kidding yourself about why you made it. We sometimes do things for a different reason than we lead ourselves to believe.

When you make a conscious choice and follow that choice up by asking yourself why you made the choice, you begin to understand a great deal more about yourself and why you do what you do. You begin to give yourself some of the important clues that help you answer the question, "Who am I really, and what do I really want?"

Practicing Choice-Thinking Controls Procrastination

Choice-Management would have a great impact in some people's lives if it did nothing more than help them get *procrastination* under control.

Being aware of your choices does a lot more than that, of course, but procrastination is almost always the direct result of failing to manage your choices.

Let's say that it is Saturday afternoon and it's time to water the lawn. It's not a big job; it takes only a few minutes to go outside, set up the sprinkler, and turn on the faucet. But it is a task that has been easily put off now and then over the past few weeks and the lawn is starting to show it.

The thought comes to mind, "I should water the

lawn." In the past, the next thought has been, "I'll do it later." But this time, you say, *"Is this a choice?"* (Yes, it is.) You then say, *"This is my choice."* And then, *"My choice is . . ."* (The choices are: 1. To water the lawn. 2. To not water the lawn.) And then, you complete the process by saying, *"My reason for my choice is . . ."* and complete the sentence.

Try that with the next minor opportunity for procrastination that comes your way and watch what happens. Keep handy your 3 × 5 card with the four steps written down on it, and go through each step, reading them out loud or saying them silently to yourself, and go through the process. Do your best not to put it off.

At first, your old programs—those that got you to *believe* that you are a procrastinator—may try to fight the new idea and tell you that it won't work. But keep doing it, every chance you get. Each time it works *for* you, you will be creating an important new "I take action!" program in your subconscious mind.

In time, enough of those new programs will get together, and could help you make a very important change in one of the basic parts of your behavior—now you get things done.

If you would like to get things done, becoming a Choice-Thinker can make a big difference in helping you get there.

Follow the Four Steps of Choice

Imagine the effect that getting into the habit of following those four simple "steps of choice" could have in your life. If you make a point of asking yourself those four questions every time the opportunity comes up, this is what you will be doing for yourself:

1. You will be more aware of your choices.

The real secret to making choices is in the *recognition* that we are making choices in the first place. When you ask yourself the question, "Is this a choice?" you put yourself in touch with yourself and with the choices you would really like to make.

2. You develop a habit of letting yourself know that the choice is yours.

When you say to yourself, "This choice is mine," you begin to program yourself not only to recognize how many choices are really yours to make in the first place, but you give yourself the program that tells you: "I take responsibility to make choices for myself."

There is no freedom quite like the freedom of recognizing that you make choices for yourself. But that freedom is a habit that you have to create and practice for yourself. Exercising the right to say, "This choice is mine" at every opportunity helps you create the habit.

3. You will always know what your choices are.

When you state your choices in clear, simple words out loud or to yourself, you will always know what your choices really are. That not only leaves the responsibility of making choices for yourself up to you, but it helps you to recognize and understand the choices that you make.

When you state to yourself, "My choice is . . .", you will automatically feel the positive effects of taking that responsibility. *You're* doing it. *You* are making the decision. *You* are creating the choices that affect and direct your life. When you do that, you feel good about it! You have something to feel *proud* of.

There is perhaps no better programming you can give yourself than the programming that tells you that you approve of yourself—you like what you are doing, and you are proud of yourself for doing it.

4. You will learn to become aware of why you make the choices you make.

In the past, many of the choices that each of us made, as we have learned, were the result of our past programming. It was as though those choices were up to *them* instead of *us*. Now *you* are in control of your choices. You are aware of the choices you make, and you know why you make them.

That is a picture of a person who is in control.

Each time you ask yourself the question, "Why did I choose to make this choice?" you force yourself to give yourself good reasons for the choices you make. That can be a challenge, but it is worth the time that it takes to ask yourself the question and give yourself a good answer.

Each time you do this, you give yourself more personal control over each choice you make—and doing that always gives you more control over what happens to you in your life.

Again:

1. Ask yourself, *"Is this a choice?"*
2. Say to yourself, *"This choice is mine."*
3. State the words, *"My choice is . . ."* and complete the sentence.
4. Ask yourself the question, *"Why have I made this choice?"*

As it is with most of our successes in life, it is often the simplest of the steps we take that make the difference. These four steps are simple enough, and they work. The results they create for people, when they begin using them, are sometimes surprising—and *always* worthwhile.

"The choices we make in the heat of emotion would be better if left for some other day."

17

CONTROLLING THE EMOTIONAL CHOICE

SOMETIMES WE MAKE STRONG CHOICES that seem right at the time but later prove to be wrong. Heading the list of these are the choices made for us or controlled by our emotions.

Choices we make under the influence of strong emotions seldom have the objectivity our other choices have. That's because strong emotions flip more of our mental "switches"—they create more chemical and electrical activity in the brain, and those highly charged thought patterns literally override or overpower other more logical thought patterns.

The result is that you may have all of the logic, reasoning and information necessary to make a good choice, but when emotion steps in, if it is strong enough, the "emotional choice" takes over. It can cause you to make the wrong choice.

It is interesting that while most of us recognize better choices are made with a calm, cool head, even though we know better than to let ourselves get out of control, we will now and then, while we are emotional, make choices we end up regretting later. It is one of the rules of the programming process of the subconscious mind that the strength of the program is influenced by the amount of emotion associated with it. The greater the chemical and electrical activity in the brain associated with the thought or program, the greater the chance that the program will be stronger than programs that are less electrically active in the brain.

It is like the difference between a program command shouted to you (high energy programming) and a program command quietly whispered to you (low energy programming). Which of the two programming commands is likely to get your attention? The strongest program, of course.

If you have a strong emotional program pushing you in one direction while you would rather be following the cool, calm, logical advice from quieter programs that are nudging you from the other direction, it may be difficult for objectivity to win out. It isn't your fault, of course; that's how the brain operates—the strongest program wins.

The Real Reason Why Love Is Blind

If you understand how this programming process works in the brain, you can begin to see why the notion that "love is blind" is not just the observation of poets; it is based on physiological paths and patterns in the brain. It is also easy to understand why, when we are in love and making some of the choices that we make, that other people look at us and shake their heads. They know better.

But then, at the moment, their programming isn't going through a massive amount of electrical and chemical excitement that is generated by our *feelings*. Of *course* they know better. Their everyday decision-making circuitry isn't being overridden by this energy-charged mental electricity we call love.

Most of us have either experienced this ourselves or watched it happen with others. And when it happens to us, we feel almost powerless to do anything about it. Few of us seem to be able to control the emotional choice.

The daughter of a friend of mine dropped out of

college during her senior year to be with a young man with whom she had fallen in love. Dropping out of school was not necessarily the logical thing to do. Leaving school, leaving town and moving a thousand miles away, getting a job, and struggling at starting a home life may not have been an objective choice. Then why did she make that choice?

Her emotional programs were stronger than all of the more logical, objective programs that were stored in the programming files of her subconscious mind. That's not what the poets tell us; but that *is* what happens.

I know a man who lives alone. A number of years ago, the light of his life, his wife, passed away. In his grief and solitude, he came to the conclusion that he would never be happy again, that he would find no one else, and that there was no reason to try. His choice, to live in solitude, may not be at all logical. There could be, if he chose differently, an exceptionally fulfilling life in front of him. But the emotions created by his loss were so great that the programs those emotions formed in his mind have overridden and overpowered every other program to the contrary for over seven years.

I'm not suggesting that emotional choices are necessarily the wrong ones to make. It is, without any doubt, by the vitality of our own emotions that we overcome the odds, reach our greatest potentials, and fuel the incredible surge of life within us. While some families have been pulled apart because of the emotional choice of someone in the relationship, other families have pulled together, built and prospered, because of that same emotion.

But our emotions are a driving force, and those emotions can create programs which can override the programs that should be guiding the best of our choices.

Choices of Anger

There is probably no clearer example of emotional choices that get in our way than those we make in anger. It is while we are angry that we say and do things that clearly work against us even while we *know* we are making the wrong choices *even while we are making them.* I have seen parents in a fit of anger shout or say things to their children that are wrong and harmful—and the parent knows it, but feels powerless to stop. That is *emotion* controlling *choice.*

I have known good people who would lose their objectivity, common sense, and any sign of maturity, just because someone said something to them that made them angry. I once saw a grown man nearly get into a fight with another adult because he thought the other man had stepped in front of him in a ticket line for a movie. The other man had merely joined his wife, who was already waiting in line.

I remember one woman whose prize possession was her long, beautiful hair. It was also a great source of pride to her husband, and he often commented on how beautiful her hair was. Then, because of an emotion-charged argument with her husband, she had her hair cut off. No more than hours later, she missed it and so did he. It wasn't an intelligent thing to do; it was an *emotional* thing to do. Her program of anger overrode her program of common sense.

As a boy, I remember playing baseball near the irrigation canal, a steep ditch with high, sloping sides and a long drop to the water below. One day, the kid who owned the baseball got mad at us and threw his ball in the canal. There was no way to retrieve the ball, and it was the only ball we had to play with, so we couldn't play anymore until one of us talked our parents into buying a new one.

As an adult, I still meet people—seemingly grown-up, mature and sensible people—who are still throwing the baseball into the canal. It doesn't make any sense, but the program of anger is often stronger than every other program we have that would ask us to think, take some time, be a little more mature, and make a better choice.

I met a man recently who literally walked off the job,

not because of the job itself, but because of something someone said to him while he was at work. He needed the work, and he could not afford to lose the job. A day or two later, after giving the matter some thought, he wished he could get his old job back. But by then his pride had gotten in the way and he wasn't going to humble himself and admit that he had made a mistake. By the time he finally got around to talking to his boss about getting his job back, his job was gone.

His first choice was made for him by *anger*. His second choice was made for him by *pride*. There may be nothing wrong with either of those two emotions, but when those emotions made that man's choices for him, it was his *emotions* that were setting his path through life; it was the man's emotions that were determining his future—not him!

One woman I met at a seminar told me that her two grown sisters had not talked to each other for over five years—all because of an argument they had had—and neither of them could remember exactly what started the argument in the first place!

The point here is not that we should be critical of people for the emotional choices they make—we *all* let our emotions make our choices for us from time to time. But until we choose to take control of the emotions that control us, we are not really in control at all. We may do fine, make good choices, and get our lives working and running on an even keel until our emotions step in again and say, "We're back, and we're in charge!"

Choices of Fear

Fear is an emotion that can fool us. It can be there without us even recognizing that it is there. Most of us would probably find it surprising to learn just how many things we do *not* do or how many things we do because of unconscious fears and insecurities.

You have probably known someone who did not get a raise or a promotion at work because they were unconsciously afraid to ask for one. Not asking for the promotion was not a logical, objective choice. It was a choice that was made almost entirely by the emotion of insecurity or hidden fear.

I wonder sometimes what we as humans could accomplish in any one lifetime if we could simply get past this one common problem of human behavior; we let the programmed emotions of fear and insecurity make too many of our choices for us. And because fear and insecurity are *emotional* programs, they are strong programs—and all too often, they become the programs that create the choices that win out, when a confident, practical, secure choice would have been a far better one to make.

How many times do we fail to make the choice to do something new, or different, or challenging because we fear failing if we try? Our somewhat experienced, reasonably well-organized mind tells us, "You can do this. This one is possible; you have what it takes. I suggest you go for this." Those are good programs to have, and we all have some of them. But then another set of programs steps in and tells us, "You can't do this. You don't have what it takes. You'll look foolish when you fail. Why even try?"

I know people who won't go swimming in a public place because they are afraid of how they will look. But the fear is only in the mind of the individual who refuses to go swimming.

There are even groups of popular fears that make our choices for us, ones not even beginning to approach the level of phobias. There are tens of thousands of individuals whose choices of how and when and where they travel are almost entirely determined by their fear of flying. And there are hundreds of thousands of completely capable, calm and collected individuals who would endure almost anything rather than have to stand up and speak in front of a group.

That is not logical, nor is it reasonable. As many people as I have seen speak in front of audiences, I have never yet seen a single audience turn on the speaker and try to lynch him or pull him off the stage. So why do we make the choice to avoid, at almost any cost, standing in front of the group and speaking? Because the emotional choice outweighs the logical choice. We *know* that the speaking cannot harm us, yet we *feel* afraid or insecure.

How Do We Put Ourselves in Control?

When I ask this question at a seminar, after discussing the emotions that control our choices, one of the first answers I get is that in order to control an emotional choice, you have to learn to be more logical and objective. The other answer I hear most often is that in order to control emotional choices, you have to first learn to control your emotions.

I would agree that in most cases, both of those ideas make sense. But let's take them one at a time and see if these solutions really work.

1. Learn to control your emotional choices by learning to be more logical and objective.

Some of the most logical and objective people you will ever meet make some of the most important choices of their lives based on their emotions and not on their ability to reason. And when we understand that emotional programs create stronger activity in the brain, it is easy to understand why.

Does that mean that you cannot overrule emotion with logical choice? No, it doesn't. If you work at it hard enough, make enough choices of reason, and give those choices plenty of mental energy to back them up, you can, if you choose, override the emotional choice. And, the more you do it, the easier it will become. This is because some of your past programming of emotional choices becomes displaced by new programs which are stronger because you are repeating them more often and giving them more energy—thus they become the stronger programs.

But unless you work at this consciously and actively

for a period of time, and concentrate some energy on controlling your emotional choices—by your own *choice*—it is likely that your emotional choices will remain the same, just as strong as ever. *The first step in taking control is to become aware of the choices you make that are energized by your emotions.* Becoming aware of the choices you make and why you make them is one of the most important steps you can take.

2. Learn to control your emotional choices by learning to control your emotions.

Most of us *do* know someone who has learned to control his or her emotions. But you probably know a number of other people who may *never* get firmly in control of their emotions.

There are also many parts of our emotional makeup that we may not *want* to control—who would want to put a limit on feeling love or joy, as an example? And yet, love and joy create choices for us that we sometimes later wish we had made differently.

The answer is that there are times when you *should* use more of the reasoning skills you spent so many years developing. And there are times that you *should* control a "harmful" emotion, such as inappropriate anger that gets in your way. Your conscious choice to make good objective choices built on experience and good common sense—if you act on it—could be one of the most worthwhile and rewarding choices that you will ever make.

Your decision to keep your emotions in check, letting your positive emotions work for you while at the same time putting yourself firmly in control of negative ones that have been working against you in the past, can do wonders in helping to create peace, stability, and emotional well-being in your life.

If you want to put yourself more in control and give less energy to unconscious or unwanted emotional choices in your life, there are two choices that will help. Simply stated, they are:

1. When I make choices, I choose to be reasonable and objective.

2. When I make choices, I choose to be in control of my emotions.

The next time an emotion starts to get in the way of making a good choice, repeat those two choices out loud or over and over to yourself until they become the strongest programs in your mind while you are making the choice.

You may not immediately sweep away the anger or the fear or the other emotion that you are feeling at the moment, but you will be making yourself vitally aware that the results of the choice you are about to make are the results that you would most like to live with long after the emotion and particular situation are gone.

There is one other choice that can help you not only control your emotional choices, but help you make better choices at any time, in any circumstance. It is called "the intuitive choice."

"Listen to the quietest whispers of your mind.

■

They are telling you the choices that will help you the most."

18

THE INTUITIVE CHOICE

No THOROUGH LOOK at the subject of choices would be complete without a close look at one of the most interesting facets of human personality—human intuition. What we call "intuition" may play an incredibly important role in the choices we make—and if it doesn't, it should.

But intuition is misunderstood; there are many myths about it. And it has been only recently that even those in the field of human motivation and behavior have begun to understand what intuition really is and how it works.

What is this curious aspect of mind that plays such an important role—or at least *tries* to play a role—in the making of our choices? What is that quiet, small voice inside us that tries to get our attention and so often fails? And where does it come from?

Few capabilities of the human brain and mind have been accorded such a mystical position as intuition. It is a curious part of our intellect that has been given an almost spiritual quality by writers and philosophers throughout the ages.

As many believe, there may well be higher spiritual forces that guide and direct us; and there are those who

would present us with what they believe to be proof of
that spiritual guidance playing a role in their individual
lives. But intuition is not the result of some mystical
guiding force. And when viewed in the light of our more
recent understanding of the programming process of the
human brain, intuition emerges as an important new tool
for us to use in the making of choices.

We are not speaking here of what some call "psychic
intuition," or knowing something we could not know by
normal means. We are speaking here of that voice each
of us has within us that often tries to get our attention
and fails, that sometimes gets through, that we occasionally listen to, and that appears to be—when it comes to
our own well-being—almost always correct.

What we call intuition is, in actuality, made up of the
programs within us that are designed to protect us. These
programs send messages of survival and fruition from our
primary genetic selves to our conscious operating person-
alities. The earliest of these "intuitive" programs may,
in fact, be spawned directly by our genetic codes.

But as we grow from infancy to adulthood, those
early programs of self-protection, survival, fruition and
fulfillment attract other similar programs from our expe-
riences and our conditioning from others. In time, these
individual programs begin to form a set of directions:
they tell us what is good for us and what is not, what will
work and what probably won't, what we should do and
what we shouldn't, what will harm us and what will help
us.

These programs of intuition become some of the
most important ones we possess, because they are designed to help us make only the best possible choices.

It is an interesting curiosity of our society that in
spite of our growing understanding of the human brain
and mind, it has become almost popular to ignore our
own intuition, one of humankind's most important mental
capabilities.

Instead of recognizing intuition as a set of highly
important, protective programs that help us make better

choices, we have confused the concept of intuition with a misleading and completely inaccurate jumble of myths.

Modern Myths About Human Intuition

Let's look at some of the things many people believe *today* about intuition.

1. Some people have it; some people don't.

Untrue. Intuition is part of the natural programming process of the human brain—everyone has it. We are born with the building blocks for the development of programmed intuition already set in place. Some people may exercise their "intuitive skills" more than others, and thereby get more use from their programs of intuition, but *everyone* has intuitive programming. It is part and parcel of human life.

2. Women have more intuition than men.

Untrue. It may be generalized that women *listen* more carefully to these programs than do men, but even that speculation appears to change based on social styles and cultures. We all have intuition. Some just listen better than others.

3. Intuition is an accident and happens by chance.

This also is untrue. Intuition is a facet of our programming and happens as a natural result of the physiological functioning of the human brain.

4. Intuition cannot be controlled.

Like any set of programs that direct or support us, the recognition of intuitive "messages" is something that can be practiced and enhanced. Members of certain religious orders and students of certain forms of meditation and mental stimulation have done this for thousands of years. We have more recently, however, learned that listening to the sometimes quiet voice of our own intuition is not a transcendental experience; it is a very natural but often ignored facet of the human mind.

5. Objective choices are more trustworthy than following intuition.

This may be only partially true. When looked at over a long period of time, the best choices you will make will probably be those that use a *combination* of objectivity and intuition. Your intuition may not always be correct, but it is always based on programs that are designed to protect you.

(I should add that the intuition we are discussing is not at all like the kind of hunch that might tell you to bet your entire life's savings on a roll of the dice. That's not intuition—that's an unconscious desire for wish fulfillment.)

The reason the subject of intuition is so important to the subject of making choices is that our own intuition could (and would, if we would let it) help us make so many more of the *right* choices—without always having to learn the right choice the hard way after we failed to make it in the first place. It has been said that the reason we have to learn so much by experience is because we fail to listen to our intuition.

When you are making a choice of any importance or substance, it doesn't really take any longer to ask yourself the simple question, "Is this really right for me? What is really the best for my total well-being—not only for today, but for my very best future?"

I suspect that if more of us in our society actually asked ourselves those questions, listened to the real answers, and then made our choices, we would have fewer problems in our lives.

If It's That Important, Why Don't We Listen?

If our intuition is actually a special set of programs that are trying desperately to protect us—and if those programs are that *important*—why aren't they louder, why don't we hear them, or why don't we listen?

Once again, strong programs win out. Our day-to-day programs governing our life at work and at home, our personal relationships and our financial demands and other responsibilities all shout to get our attention. Some days, each new mental message that we hear demands more of our attention than the last one. Kids, work, the boss, television, worries, doubts, goals, problems, challenges, responsibilities . . . all vie for our mental energies and attention.

In the days of a simpler life, the quiet truths that were spoken to us by our minds were easier to hear. But the fact remains that whatever you choose to give your attention to is what you will hear—regardless of the mental competition from other programs.

If you want to hear the voice of the programs that were designed to help you, protect you, and to always see to it that you are doing what is right and best for you, the programs and the messages are already there and waiting to be heard.

How many times, much later, after you had made the wrong choice, have you said to yourself, "I knew better," or "If only I had listened to myself," or "Next time I'm going to listen"? When it comes to making the right choices in your life, I can think of no better advice.

"Even the <u>best</u> of choices is only as strong as the choices that stand by its side."

19

WINNING CHOICES
NEVER STAND ALONE

A MAN I KNEW told me that he had made the firm decision at least a dozen times in half as many years to get on his feet financially. He wanted to have more money in the bank, and he wanted to get a better job, one that would give him the income he needed to reach his financial goals.

Each time during those several years that he made the firm choice to improve his financial position, he was completely sincere. It was a worthwhile goal; it was something that would benefit him and his family, and it was something he very badly wanted to accomplish.

The man had what appeared to be all of the right ingredients put together to make a good choice and make it work. And yet, as determined as he was, the end of each month found him with no more than his normal savings in the bank, not much further ahead than he was the month before, and not any closer to reaching his real goal of financial security or independence. He had made a good choice, but why didn't it work?

A young woman had her heart set on placing in her city's local 10K run. She made the choice not only to run, but to run as one of the leading contenders. In order to accomplish the goal, she also made the choice to train by running daily for months in advance. She put herself on an appropriate diet and made the choice to give up other activities that would interfere with her workout schedule. She spent time with other runners who had done well in the past, and she gave herself small rewards along the way when she had followed her regimen faithfully or reached new levels of endurance.

She entered the run along with 750 other registrants and placed in the top twenty-five. That had been her choice, and she reached her goal. Why did her choice work when the same choice made by others did not work for them?

A man began to notice that his communication with his 15-year-old daughter and 14-year-old son was starting to break down. He had been a fairly good communicator in the past, but not the best, and he was concerned about the normal changes in relationships between parents and teenage kids. So he made the choice to spend more time talking to his daughter and son.

It was an excellent parenting choice, and he had good reason to reach his objective. But less than a year later, it became clear to him that, although the goal was still just as important, he was actually communicating less and not more. He had made the choice to spend more time talking with each of them, and yet he seemed to be communicating less. What had gone wrong?

Always Give Your Choices a Team of Support

The woman who successfully ran the 10K run did something that neither the man who wanted to become financially independent nor the father of the two young teenagers understood. Instead of just making one basic, "primary" choice to define and reach her goal, she supported that choice with additional choices that worked *together* to make the first choice stronger.

When you support your *primary* choice with other choices, you create a *team* of choices. Each of them works together to support, defend and build up the others like the players on a football team. Each player has his own position to play, but all of them work together to reach the final specific objective of getting the ball across the goal line.

Let's look at a few reasonably important choices to see what team effort of additional choices might be necessary to make the primary choice work.

The choice to diet and to lose weight often fails because the primary choice is there but there are no other choices to form the team that backs it up. The choice to lose weight never stands on its own. Ask anyone who has successfully lost weight and kept it off, and they will tell you what it takes!

Here are some of the team choices that help make weight loss work.

Primary choice: *I choose to lose weight*.
Support team choices:

- The choice to eat only the right kind and amount of food.
- The choice to get the right amount and kind of exercise.
- The choice to see yourself differently (thinner and healthier).
- The choice to avoid situations that encourage poor eating habits.
- The choice to spend more time with people who encourage and support your weight-loss choices.

That's how to make losing weight a *team effort!* Instead of letting the primary choice work or fail all by itself, a team of choices supports your primary choice from every side.

I mentioned earlier the example of the father whose choice it was to spend more time talking to his teenage daughter and son. He failed in his primary choice because it did not occur to him that winning choices never stand alone. Any time you want to improve an important per-

sonal relationship, if that is your primary choice, here
are some of the team choices that will help.

Primary choice: *I choose to improve an important
personal relationship*.
Support team choices:

- The choice to devote more time to working on the
  relationship.
- The choice to practice listening and listen every
  chance you get.
- The choice to express yourself more positively.
- The choice to practice being considerate 100 per-
  cent of the time.
- The choice to never argue.
- The choice to find more common interests to
  share.
- The choice to recognize and openly show appre-
  ciation for who the other person is.

Adding these extra support team choices may look
like you're adding extra work, but just the opposite is
true. By making the extra choices, you're making your
job *easier,* not more difficult. And you are greatly in-
creasing the chances that your primary choice will work.

Another example of this is the student who makes
the choice to do better in school. Because of bad grades,
parental disapproval, or desire for personal achievement,
many students will finally make the clear, conscious
choice to do better in school. But that one choice, no
matter how important it may be, will seldom succeed
standing on its own. It needs a team of supportive choices
on its side.

Primary choice: *I choose to do better in school*.
Support team choices:

- The choice to improve study skills and habits.
- The choice to spend more time studying.

- The choice to cut down on activities that get in the way of schoolwork.
- The choice to use better concentration, listening skills, and focus in class.
- The choice to spend time with friends who are scholastically strong and supportive of your goals.
- The choice to reward yourself when you do well.
- The choice to continue regardless of difficulties along the way (determination).

The man we mentioned earlier who made the choice to improve his financial position failed to do so because he lacked team support. Here are just a few of the kinds of choices that belong on the support team for earning more income.

Primary choice: *I choose to earn more income.*
Support team choices:

- The choice to carefully examine the job you're in now (or what you are presently doing to earn your income).
- The choice to make a list of your options.
- The choice to do what it takes—training, job change, etc.
- The choice to refuse to accept less than you're worth.
- The choice to be assertive about your income.
- The choice to never again make an excuse for not earning enough.
- The choice to start setting specific goals, writing them down, and reviewing them regularly.

When someone has made the choice to improve himself, one of the first choices I often hear stated is to get more done. Choosing to actually accomplish more, day after day, for any period of time is a tall order for anyone. It can be done, of course, but it takes a team effort.

Primary choice: *I choose to get more accomplished.*
Support team choices:

- The choice to set priorities and *write them down*.
- The choice to decide what you are *not* going to do.
- The choice to keep your energy strong.
- The choice to make a plan and follow the plan.
- The choice to ask for help when you need it.
- The choice to take time off when you need to.
- The choice to give yourself a gold star every time you accomplish all the items on your daily "to do" list.

Remember, too, winning choices attract and create other winning choices. The choices you make will help you determine and focus on the objectives you want to reach. The extra choices you put on your team will help you get there.

"It is the big choices we make that set our direction.

■

It is the smallest choices we make that get us to the destination."

20

THE CHOICES
IN THE LANGUAGE
OF SELF-TALK

A NUMBER OF YEARS AGO I began writing the first of many Self-Talk scripts to be recorded on cassettes. These scripts consisted of a selection of Self-Talk phrases. Each script included about fifteen or twenty phrases covering one individual subject area.

Over the years I wrote and recorded a collection of more than two thousand Self-Talk phrases that covered dozens of personal improvement subject areas.

During that time I received letters from many individuals who were finding that reading Self-Talk phrases, or listening to those same phrases on cassette tapes, made a noticeable and lasting difference in their attitudes and actions.

We learned from new findings in the study of the human brain, why the use of Self-Talk should work "physiologically." And we learned from countless Self-Talk users that using the repeated phrases of Self-Talk worked in practice as well. But it was after the use of Self-Talk had already started to become popular that I began to understand *why* Self-Talk was working so well.

Using Self-Talk Helps Make Choices

The breakthrough finally came while I was appearing on a live television broadcast in which viewers were calling in to the program to ask questions about the subject of Self-Talk.

One of the questions many people have when they first learn about Self-Talk is the way Self-Talk phrases are worded.

The phrases of Self-Talk are worded in a very specific way. They are always stated in the *first person*, *present tense*, and a typical Self-Talk phrase about earning more money or doing better financially would sound like this: "I always earn more than I need. I am financially secure and grow financially stronger each and every day."

A dozen or more phrases of that nature, recorded together, and repeated in a specific way on your own or on a Self-Talk cassette, and played two or three times each day, has proved to have strong positive effects on both the financial *attitude* and on the financial *position* of the person using the Self-Talk.

During the television talk show, a viewer called in who was not familiar with Self-Talk. Her question was, "How can I listen to a cassette tape of Self-Talk that tells me things about myself in the present tense as though they were already true, when I know they're not true yet?"

Her problem was that since Self-Talk is recorded in the present tense, when you first listen to Self-Talk it may contain phrases which do not apply to you now.

But there is an important reason why Self-Talk is phrased in this way—it is simply to give the subconscious the most complete, accurate picture of what you *choose* to have happen.

Self-Talk is phrased in this way because the subconscious mind responds to programs which are the clearest and strongest. It would do little or no good to give yourself Self-Talk which diluted your self-directions with words like, "I'm going to," or "I'd like to," or, "In the future I will . . . ," etc.

Because of time limitations on the television show, I wanted to give as clear and simple an answer as possible without going into any great detail on the programming processes of the subconscious mind.

So in answering the question I said, "Look at each Self-Talk phrase as a choice, if you like. If you're working at being a better money manager and you have trouble with the idea of saying, "I always manage my money well," just add the words, "I *choose to* always manage my money well." That's what you're really saying: "This is how I choose to be. This is how I am becoming. This is how I really am." This is how you create a Self-Talk for any situation.

I did not realize at the moment that I had happened upon the final reason why Self-Talk works so well: *Self-Talk helps manage the choices you have made plus helps you make new, positive ones by creating positive programs in the brain to help you make good new choices.*

A short time later I reread many of the Self-Talk scripts which I had originally written. A careful examination of those Self-Talk scripts confirmed my hypothesis. *Every Self-Talk statement is a directive to the subconscious mind that says,* "This is my choice—this is what I choose."

And *choices* create *programs* in the brain.

New Choices Create New Programs

At that time I realized the concept of Self-Talk had finally come full circle. We had known, even before the development of Self-Talk in its present form, that it is our *choices* that lie at the root of our successes and failures in life.

We learned that the reason we so often *limited* ourselves, was because we had mental programs that gave us inaccurately pessimistic pictures of our potential.

With Self-Talk, we learned that many of those programs could be turned around. We learned that we could override or replace old, negative programs with new programs of our choosing. Programs that would help us see ourselves in a much better light and help us create the self-picture—and self-esteem—necessary to lead a more fulfilling life.

Eventually we also began to understand that just as our old programming was helping us make poor choices, our new choices were creating *new* programs within us. As we discussed in an earlier chapter, our poor programming in the past has created poor choices for many of us. But *new choices*—that we make *now*—also create *new programs*.

It was the final link in this chain of Self-Management that would bring us back to where we started.

Self-Talk is a way of making conscious, specific choices, which create new programs in the brain that override or replace previous negative programs, which had given us poor choices to begin with.

The conclusion is, *"Good Self-Talk creates good choices, which create good programs, which create good Self-Talk, which creates good choices . . . etc., etc., etc." And so an incredible cycle of powerful, positive Self-Management begins.*

Learning the Words of Choice

If you are not yet familiar with the phrasing and use of Self-Talk, here is an example of a popular Self-Talk script entitled, "Setting and Reaching Goals." Notice the *choices* that are stated in the following Self-Talk phrases:

- I set goals. I write them down and review them often.
- My goals give me a clear picture of my own positive future—in advance!
- I spend several minutes each day reviewing the goal cards I write for myself. I read my goals to myself each morning when I awake, and each night just before I go to sleep.
- My goals are very specific. The more detailed and specific they are, the more clearly I am able to visualize them and create them in my life.

- Every time I see something in myself that I choose to change, or decide on something that I want in my life, I write it down, set a goal, review it daily, act on it, and achieve it.

- My goals are my road map to my own future. I plan where I am going, how I will get there, and when I will arrive.

- I am successful when I achieve my goals, but I am also successful each day of the journey. I know that success lies not only at the end of the road, but in each step along the way.

- I set daily goals, weekly and monthly goals, and goals that set my sights for a year or more in front of me.

- By setting short-term, medium and long-range goals, I stay in touch with where I am today, and I give positive, active direction to where I will be tomorrow.

- I take absolute responsibility for who I am and where I'm going. By setting goals and working daily to achieve them, I take responsibility for determining my own destiny.

- I choose to live my life by choice, not by chance. Setting goals and working to reach them keeps me in control of my life.

- I consciously make the decisions that affect my life and my future in the most positive, possible way.

- Anytime I want to make a change or achieve anything in my life, I write it down, along with my plan to accomplish the goal and when I will achieve it. In this way I turn each of my goals into action.

- By writing out my goals, I am actually writing my own script for the story of my future. By following my specific action plan, I turn my dreams into reality.

Setting the Process in Motion

As you can see from this simple script of Self-Talk phrases, *every statement of Self-Talk is a CHOICE!*

To show you how the Self-Management cycle works, let's take just one of the phrases from that script and walk it through the process from early programs to final choices.

For our example, we'll use the Self-Talk phrase, "I set goals. I write them down, and I review them often."

Let's say your early program did not create any real interest in setting goals and over the years you have set goals only occasionally, but have not made a real issue of goal-setting, and have not put a lot of conscious time and effort into the practice. Goal setting, therefore, has not been a priority.

When the choice comes up to list your goals, set specific target dates for reaching your goals and reviewing those goals frequently, the likely choice will be not to do it. That choice is the result of your previous programming.

Each time you make the negative choice, you are giving yourself another new program that reinforces and duplicates the old negative programs about setting and reaching goals.

It is easy to see how the cycle takes place and continually builds on itself. Unless something happens to break the cycle and change the pattern, it will continue.

Past negative *programs* create negative *choices* in the *present!* Those negative choices create *new negative programs*. And *those* negative programs create *more* negative *choices,* which in turn *create more new negative programs of the same kind*.

But now let's say *you* decide to change the pattern. To begin with, let's assume that you have early negative programming about setting and reaching goals and that your choices in the past have been to follow the old programming and spend very little conscious time and effort working at setting goals and reviewing them.

But now it's time to make the change.

One way you may begin is by listening to a cassette tape of the Self-Talk phrases for setting and reaching goals. Or, you can create your own phrases. Each of the phrases you hear on the cassette (or read or repeat to yourself from a written list) now becomes a new *choice*.

And each of the new choices are specific self-directions, which you are consciously and clearly delivering to your subconscious mind.

You are now saying, "These are my choices. These are my *new* choices about setting and reaching goals. These are the new directions I want you to follow."

With that message now being delivered over and over to the subconscious mind (by using your new Self-Talk repeatedly), the new choices you are giving yourself begin to create *a new set of programs* in your mind.

In time, the *new* programs begin to override your earlier, negative goal-setting programs, and the new programs take over.

Now let's step ahead a few weeks or months into the future. An opportunity comes up which clearly calls for the setting of goals.

In order to do it right, you will need to write your goals down on paper, review them frequently, and follow a specific action plan which will help you put the new goals into effect.

Given enough of the repeated programming that your new *choices* of Self-Talk gave you, what do you suppose your new choice about setting and reaching goals will be?

And, if your new choice gets you to set the goal, work on it, and see it through to completion, what do you suppose the successful achievement of that goal will create in your subconscious mind?: *A successful new program—and new mental energy for making more good choices*.

The old cycle works like this:

- The old program creates a negative choice.
- The negative choice creates new programs of the same negative kind.

- The additional new negative programs create more negative choices.

The new cycle works like this:

- The old programs (if they are negative) create negative choices.
- You decide by conscious *choice* (right now, as an example) to give yourself some clear, strong, new choices.
- You use conscious, positive Self-Talk to create the new choices.
- The new choices, from the new Self-Talk you have created, *form new programs in the brain* that override the old, negative choice programs.
- The new programs now take off on their own and deliver a better set of choices to you.
- Each time you make a newer, better choice, you create another positive program in your mind, and your healthier new cycle of programming and choices is off and running.

A few years ago, when I was spending most of my time writing about the subject of Self-Talk, doing nonstop radio and television tours, and discussing Self-Talk in seminars and lectures, I knew that we had finally found an answer to self-programming that worked. But I also thought that with the discovery of Self-Talk as we know and use it today, there were probably no "Ah-ha's" left.

I was wrong. Self-Talk was just the beginning. Self-Talk would prove to be an important part of *a whole new way to make choices!* And those choices would prove to be the single most powerful and important key in the master control mechanism that runs our lives.

If you would like to make specific choices that put

you in charge of your own programming, I would recommend that you use your own Self-Talk to help reinforce you. Practicing the right kind of Self-Talk does more than give you a new way to direct your thoughts and make your day work better. *The Self-Talk you create helps manage the choices you make.*

"Each day that passes, your choices will come and go.

They are like diamonds in a chest of jewels, each waiting to be discovered."

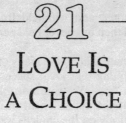

21

LOVE IS
A CHOICE

SOMETIMES WE THINK that the more profound choices— the larger choices in life—are more difficult to make than others, when in fact they are actually more simple. They are simple because they don't start with the question of whether you want them or not.

For example, I have never met anyone who did not want love, success, or happiness—at least in some degree. But I have also known people who never seemed to really find them or hold onto them in their lives.

What is it that creates love for one and withholds it from another? Why is one person "successful" in life, while another is not? Why do some people find happiness day after day, while others fail to find it, or never have enough of it?

It's Not Up to Chance—It's Up to Choice

I have heard people say that they are "unlucky in love" or that they weren't born "successful," or others who were happy only now and then.

Instead of love, success, and happiness being a natural and expected part of everyday life, many people come to believe that these three qualities are gifts from fate—given to some and withheld from others—to be enjoyed now and then but never held permanently in their hands.

It is unfortunate that all too many of us never learned when we were young that love, success, and happiness don't depend on fate. We were not told that they, too, are choices—that the achievement of each of them depends almost entirely on the choices we make.

- Love is a choice.
- Success is a choice.
- Happiness is a choice.

Of all the choices that you or I will ever make, these three choices control or give power to all the rest of our choices.

Some people choose to accept them and others don't. To choose love you have to believe you are capable of finding it; to choose success you have to believe you deserve it; to choose happiness you have to believe that it is there and that it belongs to you already.

Who—or What—Is Responsible for Your Fulfillment?

If, instead of recognizing your control over these three simple yet important choices, you believe that fate is in charge, you will tend to leave the responsibility of your own achievement up to the whims of the world around you. Instead of taking responsibility for yourself, you leave it in the hands of others.

I have never known a single truly fulfilled individual who did not take *personal* responsibility for his or her fulfillment. They never leave the important or the minor achievements of "self" up to chance—they decide what they want, they earnestly believe that they deserve the best, and they act on their decision to achieve.

When You State It, You Create It

If you said every day of your life, "I choose to be successful today, I choose to have love today, and I choose to be happy today," you would have more success, more love, and more happiness in your life. When you state it, you create it—not in some metaphysical way but in a very real way. To state it is almost to demand it. It's like saying, "Open Sesame" to open the door to the treasures that lie within.

If you don't state it, if you don't demand it, the door doesn't open, and you stand by wondering while others all around you seem to be able to open their life's treasures and live them out.

Let's find out how you can achieve three of life's greatest treasures for yourself. Let's look at the three choices of love, success, and happiness and find out what makes them happen—what makes them work.

Love Is a Choice

I have worked and written in the field of human potential long enough to know that I would never try to define for my readers what "love" is. It has many meanings, and I will leave it up to the philosophers, the saints and the poets to define it.

But we have learned something about finding it and having it. We have learned that for all its complexities, the attainment of love is ultimately a choice that each of us must make for ourselves.

What We Learned to Believe About Love

Most of us learned to believe that love is something that happens *to* us. When it is "right," it descends upon us, captures our heart, awakens our soul, and creates a magical quality in our minds that heightens our senses, excites our imagination, gives us passion, and allows us the ability to see the world in a bright and promising way.

If, when we were young, we were given a reasonably positive picture of life and what was in store for us, we learned to believe that is the way love should be.

When we were old enough, we experienced for ourselves some of what "love" was supposed to be. But in time that magic potion lost some of its magic.

The Realities of Everyday Living

In time, our early dreams of unending bliss often give way to the realities of everyday living. Our expressions of love in candlelight and moonlight bow to more practical considerations of jobs, careers, and household maintenance. And the incredibly important human need to love and be loved takes second place to car payments, shopping for groceries, and getting to work on time.

There is nothing wrong with that, of course. We do need to make car payments, shop for groceries, and get to work on time. But when we allow ourselves to be caught up in the routine of day-to-day activities, we lose contact with an essential part of who we are. We live out our lives without a sense of real purpose, and we never quite achieve the full potential for love that we somehow sense we were born with.

I'm not suggesting that the great love of life, the love we were born to deliver and to receive, is naturally diminished by a good life well lived. But it may be true that by giving in to dealing with the necessities of everyday life, we often confine or ignore the passion for living that those early feelings of love created in us in the first place.

That love failed to blossom and grow, overcome the obstacles, and withstand the test of time—not because of fate or the circumstances of life, but because someone failed to recognize that love is *always* a choice.

I doubt that anyone could calculate the number of relationships that did not work simply because someone in that relationship did not make the decision to make it work. It was a choice, but he didn't know it was a choice—or she didn't know it was a choice.

Believing Is Becoming

One man I knew told me he could never make a marriage work. He had proved in three failed marriages that what he believed was true. In his first marriage, he felt he was not right for the woman he had married, and for that reason, the marriage didn't work. In his second marriage, he believed that the woman was not right for him. That marriage didn't work either.

By his third marriage, he had become convinced what his early programs had taught him about his "inability" to love was true—that it would destroy that relationship as well. It did.

He wanted to love and to be loved, but felt he could not. And not once during those years did he stop long enough to sit down and think about his choice. Every problem, every difficulty, every difference of opinion, and every goal that he and his wife did not share in common, just reinforced his internal programming that told him success in love was not for him.

In time, he accepted his programming and proved it to be true. I have often wondered what would have happened if, every morning upon awakening, he had said to himself, "I choose to love and to be loved. This is my choice."

Because he was not aware that he could consciously choose to love and be loved, he allowed earlier negative programming to work against him, and accepted a role that proved to him he would fail.

Making Love Work

Many behavioral researchers now believe that the success of a relationship is determined not by destiny but instead by the desire and decision to make the relationship work.

Granted, though some relationships seem to be "made in heaven," many are not. It is only when we separate our expectations of a "perfect relationship" from a more practical belief in a relationship that could work, that we are forced to make the decision to do everything we need to do to *make* the relationship work.

If you have a goal that is strong enough to make the relationship work, and if you really decide to like and love the other person, chances are the relationship will work better. But if, in a marriage relationship, as an example, all you do is wait for fireworks to go off and bells to ring, chances are the relationship will be short-lived.

Some people never realize how much of what they call love is entirely up to them. But liking or even loving someone else really *is* up to the individual. If you really don't want to love the other person, you will find ways to make sure that love doesn't happen. If you want to love someone else, you can.

If you want to try this out for yourself, make the decision for the next seven days to genuinely like or "love" everything the other person does and says. Making the simple decision to admire, respect and love who the other person is, and what he or she says and does, can make a profound difference in how you see that person and how well the relationship works.

If You Want Love in Your Life

It is evident from any study of human behavior that those who want to love and to be loved open themselves up to the possibility of loving and being loved. If you want love in your life, you must *choose* to have it. People who believe they do not deserve love, or they are not capable of getting it, usually have less of it in their lives. Those who make a decision to have love, have more of it.

Choose how you want to love. Choose for yourself how you want to give love, and choose *how* you will want love to come to you. If you are in a relationship and you choose to find absolute love in that way, then make that your choice. If you are still looking for the kind of love that will make you complete, then decide what you want, demand it of yourself, insist on it, and get ready for it.

Whether you love and are loved as fully as you'd like is up to you. Love *is* a choice.

"Those who choose to succeed always do better than those who never choose at all."

22

SUCCESS IS
A CHOICE

IF OUR CHOICES CAN HELP us find and hold something as important as love, it is only logical that the same mental process should also be able to lead us toward success and happiness in life.

I have often been surprised at how difficult it seems to be for so many of us to find a full measure of success in our lives. At times it seems to be easier to find reasons why we cannot attain it than it is to find a workable way to achieve it.

What about that old program that tells you, "Maybe I can't do this"? What about those tons of old self-beliefs—or rather disbeliefs—that tell you that maybe you're not cut out for the kind of success you'd really like to have?

What do you do when you believe that you ought to be able to slay the dragons and win in life, but it just doesn't seem to work out that way? After all, when we look around us, it does seem as though some people are more "destined" to succeed in life, while others seem to be able to do little more than "get by" or stay even. It is almost as though the odds just aren't in our favor.

No One Was Born to Lose

Let me give you some encouragement. No one, not one single person who was ever born on the face of this earth, was born to fail—or to automatically succeed. We tell ourselves that this person or that person was "born with a silver spoon in his mouth," but when it gets right down to it, we know better.

We have all seen people who were supposedly destined for success and somehow fail to reach it; they never really achieve anything. We have seen others who grew up in the worst possible conditions—people who seemingly had nothing at all going for them—and yet they achieved major successes in their lives.

It does, at first glance, appear to us that some people have it better than others. It certainly is true that some people seem to have more opportunities and a better chance to succeed in life. Other people seem to have the cards stacked against them.

But is that really true? It's not true at all.

All of us, when we are born, when we are infants in the cradle, have unlimited potential in front of us.

A lot of that potential, of course, gets programmed out of us at a very early age. We grow up in an environment that expects less than the best of us; we are told what we cannot do; we are persuaded by our conditioning to become "average" or *less* than average—and in time the program works.

But that doesn't diminish the potential that was there in the first place. The potential is still there for each of us.

Getting Rid of "I Can't"

You could accomplish, beginning today, almost unimaginable things in your life if you chose to. It makes no difference where you have been in the past, the problems you might have had along the way, your nurturing or lack of nurturing, your education or the lack of it, or your chances or opportunities along the way. *Your potential is still there.*

There is so much that you can do. And the only thing that is stopping you from doing "it," whatever that may be, are any negative beliefs that your programs created within you. In time, you accepted and programmed for yourself the belief that you "cannot."

So how do you get rid of the "I can't?" The answer to that question sounds almost too simple to be true: If, in the past, you have believed in what you cannot do, *stop it*. Quit believing it! Make a choice. Start believing in what you *can* do, and stop forever believing in what you *cannot* do.

No one is asking you to walk on water, transmute lead into gold, or become an overnight millionaire. No one is asking you to do the impossible. But how about asking yourself and then *telling* yourself what *is* possible? And then deciding right now to make the *choice*, and then in time a dozen choices or a hundred choices or a thousand, to *do* it.

What an incredible role our self-doubts play in our lives! They stop us, hold us back, burn bridges that we have never even crossed, and prove to us in our minds that we are, for some reason, incapable of achieving what we would like most for ourselves.

It is not the rest of the world that holds us back. It is our own disbelief in ourselves. Our own self-doubts are the demons who guard the gates of our potential and stop us from stepping through to the incredible future that stands in front of us.

From our earliest days of infancy, we learn to believe what we *cannot* do, what we *cannot* be, and what we *cannot* achieve in life. Time after time we are told what will not work, and we are left with the overwhelming burden of our limitations.

I have come to the conclusion that there must be a better way. I suspect that we may have found at least part of the answer in what we have learned about how

the human brain works—how it operates. Here is some
of what we have found.

Success Is a Choice

I was asked recently if I would write a book about
success. I declined the offer. So much has already been
written about what success is, why some have it and
others do not, and how success is there for the taking if
we will just follow the formulas. We are told that if we
follow them, success will be ours.

I agree with most of what the better authors on the
subject tell us. Their ideas are sound; their advice is
worth taking. I suspect that if a study were to be under-
taken, we would find that those who read the books and
follow the advice are generally more "successful" than
those who don't.

But it has also become apparent that those who
count themselves among the seekers of success have,
perhaps long before they listened to the advice of others
or read the books, made the *decision* to be successful.
That's why they read the books in the first place. They
had already decided that they wanted to be successful in
life, and now they were just looking for the means to
accomplish the objective.

I have known others who truly wanted success, but
try as they might, they failed to find it. Many of them still
live with the dissatisfaction of knowing that they were
close to achieving success in one form or another, but
they couldn't quite grasp it; or if they found it, it was
fleeting. They would find success for a time, and then it
would elude them again. It would be there for a while,
and then it would be gone.

For all those who still find success an important and
worthwhile goal that remains a dream—something that
will be found tomorrow or another day—the reason for
having to wait for success is that they may have not yet
chosen to have the success that they seek.

If *you* would like to make the choice to be successful,

it will help to understand some of what goes into creating our ideas about success in the first place. If you do not yet have all the success that you would like to have in your life, ask yourself the following questions and listen to your answers. They may help you find what you're looking for.

- What does success mean to you?
- Who determines your success—who do you feel is grading you now?
- What are your reasons—if any—for choosing not to be successful?
- Are you successful now without knowing it?
- Are you living for tomorrow?
- How would you describe the person you see when you look in the mirror?
- What is your choice?

You carry with you right now, in your brain, an unknown number of programs that tell you what success is. What you believe about success in life, for you or for anyone else, is based on your programming.

What Does Success Mean to You?

When you decide that you want to be successful in life, have you decided for yourself what success really means?—What it is, what it offers you, what it looks like, how it feels? If your definition of success is determined entirely by your past programming (and it is), are you sure you have the programs that give you the description of success you'd really like to have? Think about that.

Success comes in many sizes and shapes. For some, success is a series of events—successive achievements, each one of which is graded independently. Reaching a sales quota, buying a second car or paying off the first car, graduating the first child from college, getting the promotion or raise, finding the new home, putting a certain amount into the savings account each month or reaching a financial goal, losing weight, taking a college course, or getting the house and family life organized—these achievements are, in themselves, success for many of us.

For others, success is a way of life that doesn't depend on stepping stones along the way. For them, success is the destination rather than the journey.

If I were to sit down with you and ask you, "Who are you really and what do you really want?", how would you answer the question?

Who Determines Your Success— Who's Grading You Now?

Is your success in life entirely of your own choosing and determination, or are you relying on someone else to mark your score card for you? Is your success in life right now graded by your spouse or mate, your family, your relatives, your boss or your associates at work, your friends, or by acquaintances and casual observers?

None of them, of course, have any right at all to judge your success. But it is part of the habit we learned to accept others' opinions as judgments of our personal achievements. You can decide whether or not this habit is one you want to keep. Instead of allowing others to determine your success, you can, instead, take counsel with yourself. You can listen to *you!*

You are the only one who can ever determine whether you are successful or not. Taking that responsibility for yourself is an exceptional exercise in being responsible for you. The others in your life have their own successes to deal with—you have yours.

Listening to others is fine, especially when what they have to say is positive and productive, and genuinely works for you. But you alone hold the pen that writes the grades on your personal score card of success. No one else can ever come close to understanding who you really are and what you really want. When it comes right down to it, the grades you give yourself are the grades that count.

What Are Your Reasons—If Any— for Choosing Not to Be Successful?

We often give ourselves all too many reasons for not choosing success, but the truth is most of those reasons are not really reasons at all; they are simply excuses.

Over the years I have listened to countless reasons given by others for withholding success from themselves. Here are a few of them:

- "I don't have the time to do that right now."
- "I'm just not good at that."
- "I'd like to go back to school for a degree but I can't."
- "Someone else always beats me to it."
- "That's just not 'me.' "
- "Maybe someday."
- "I was always taught that . . ."
- "Some people have all the luck."
- "I'm doing okay."
- "I can't afford it."
- "Some have it and some don't."
- "I'm happy with where I am."
- "I just can't seem to get around to it."
- "I have to support my family."
- "I've got to get my kids raised first."
- "My husband (or wife) won't let me do that."
- "I'm too old/young."
- "I'm not smart enough."
- "I'm not sure I could do it."
- "If only you knew what I've been going through."
- "I have a lot of other responsibilities right now."
- "I just don't have the energy."
- "I haven't been feeling well."
- "I'm not attractive enough."
- "Too much stress."

- "What was good enough for my parents is good enough for me."
- "I'd have to make new friends."
- "I'd have to change my life-style."
- "I've never been good at . . ."
- "I don't want to take the risk."
- "I'm too shy."
- "When I lose some weight . . ."
- "They wouldn't want me."
- "I don't want to work that hard."

In the above list, the only reason that really makes sense for not choosing to be successful is the statement that says, "I'm happy with where I am." The reasons we give ourselves for putting it off and delaying our success for some other time don't even have to be good excuses—they only have to be good enough to convince us that success, for us, is for some other time.

All of the reasons for avoiding success included in that list are programs. They are beliefs that we carry within us, chemically and electrically imprinted in our brains, taught to us by others who were also longing for success but willing to put it off and hope that it would come at some other time.

All of the reasons on that list are also *choices*. And that's the good news. They may have been excuses in the past, but they are choices that you can, if you choose, turn around and make for yourself *now* in a different way.

Are You Successful Now Without Knowing It?

I have known people who were very successful and who could have enjoyed their success if they had just realized that they already had it. Because we so often allow our earlier programming to determine what success means for us, and because we allow others to mark our scorecards for us, we sometimes fail to recognize that we're already "there."

Have you ever known someone whose successes

were always in the past? The reason they do that is because they don't make the decision to choose to see their successes in the *present*.

It is only after time has passed, and they can see the clear-cut pictures of having done something that worked in the past, that they have the confidence to tell themselves that they were, at that time, successful.

Past successes may make us feel good, and they are certainly worthwhile. But most of us would agree that it feels better to recognize success *today* than to try to keep alive the wilted laurel leaves of past achievements. They are fine, of course, and it's good that we have them. But the real energy, the excitement, and the inspiration of living a successful life is always greater when we can live it in the present, now, today!

Are You Living for Tomorrow?

Some of us always seem to be living for tomorrow. We are waiting for the raise, expecting the promotion, looking forward to graduation, knowing that something good is going to happen soon, getting through a bad time and expecting things to get better, or waiting for some gold star that is yet to come that will tell us we are successful.

Yet the old adage is most certainly true: "He who waits, waits; he who doesn't, does something about it." Some people are forever waiting for the raise.

I know people who continue to tell me that something good is coming, and then, when we meet again a few months or a year or two later, they are still proclaiming something good is coming. It is unfortunate they have not yet realized that if they chose, "something good" is right now.

The present never really waits for the future. It can only happen now. There may be achievements in life that we cannot have today; but if we wait to be successful until they arrive, we stand the chance of missing out on ever seeing the sunrise of successes that tell us that today has arrived *today*.

What Do You See When You Look in the Mirror?

If we met and talked, and you asked me, "What could I do for just one year that would give me the success in my life that I want and deserve?" I would challenge you to do one thing that I knew would create more success in the years ahead than any other single thing you might do.

It would be to simply stand in front of your mirror each and every morning for the next year and tell yourself the words, "I am successful. I deserve to be successful. I *choose* to be successful."

I would not tell you what success is, nor would I give you any formula to follow to find it for yourself. I would simply tell you to say the words. You wouldn't have to say the words out loud, but you would have to think them.

When you first began saying the words, you wouldn't even have to believe them—you would just have to say them. Your brain would act on the new programming in exactly the same way whether you believed the words or not.

And in one year from today, if you had said those words each and every day without fail, I already know some of what you would tell me about what had happened in your life. There is a good chance that you would be more successful than you had been a year earlier, because the *result* of *choosing to succeed* is unavoidable.

When you choose success and decide to have it for yourself, success begins to happen.

What Is Your Choice?

What will you choose? What will you decide now or tomorrow about your success? *Those who choose to be successful tend to be more successful than those who never make the choice.*

It is, in fact, that one single important choice that will create and control a thousand other choices that you will make throughout the year ahead.

It has been proved time and again by countless individuals from every walk of life that what happens *to* us—the successes we achieve in our lives—is almost entirely up to each of us. If that is true, and I believe that it is, then the final wall standing between you and your successes in life has been nothing more than one of your own imagination—believed to be brick and mortar when it was only papier-mâché and paste.

Go ahead, make the choice. Guide yourself into your own future. It is your *choice* to be successful that makes the difference.

"The highest levels of heaven are most certainly filled with those who chose to be there."

HAPPINESS IS
A CHOICE

THE FINAL CHOICE in these three of life's most important choices is the one to be happy. This may be the most important of the three, and yet when you get good at it, it is the simplest. After carefully assessing every definition of happiness that I have found, I have come to three clear conclusions on the subject:

1. Happiness is an attitude.
2. Happiness is always up to the individual.
3. Happiness is always a choice.

Why Can't I Be Happy?

Have you ever heard someone say the words, "Why can't I be happy like other people?" or "I would be happier if only . . ." Happiness is one of those magical qualities of life that is impossible ever to have too much of. And it is certainly clear that all too many of us never get enough of it.

Why is it that happiness seems to come so easily to one and is so difficult for another to find, even when both people are in the same situation? Some have such a difficult time with this one that, in time, they come to believe there is a grand plan with a "Master Happiness List"—some people get to be on the list and some don't.

For them, happiness is all wrapped up in fate. Try as they might to find happiness for themselves, they make their way through life unhappily, convinced they will never really be happy because they believe they're not *supposed* to be. In time, they begin to resent others who are happy, and they stop looking for happiness themselves.

If we know someone who has been unhappy long enough, when we describe that person, all too often words like "bitter" and "cynical" come to mind. The color has gone out of their life. The energy, enthusiasm and excitement for living and looking forward to each grand new tomorrow are painted over in the color gray.

If happiness is, in fact, available for everyone, why is it that some have it and some don't? Is it fate, and therefore unchangeable—or is it something else entirely? The answer lies not at all in what fate has in store for us; the answer lies in what the *brain* has "stored" for us.

Happiness Is an Attitude

It is our *programming* that determines most of our happiness for us. Once again, since our attitudes are created by our beliefs, and our beliefs are created by our programming, if we want to have a better attitude about anything it helps to understand what our programs have caused us to believe about ourselves.

That information programmed in the brain creates our beliefs about everything outside of us and around us in our lives. If that was all the brain did for us, we could be in trouble, because that would mean that if we were given the wrong programs as growing children, we would be forced to live the rest of our lives with every negative program we had received along the way working against us. But the brain is designed to help us, and it wants to do so.

As we discussed earlier, we can at any time direct

our own mind any way we'd like by giving it new programs to act on. Those programs are called choices. You could, at this moment, if you chose, give yourself a different mental command or direction about any attitude you have. You would not, in a moment, change the deeper programming behind that attitude, but for now, the new *choice* would override the old *program*. The new attitude would override the old.

As an example, let's say that Jim's job makes him unhappy. He doesn't feel he's getting anywhere; his job is giving him none of the fulfillment that he needs, and because of his attitude, he is even unable to get along well with his associates at work.

Now let's say that Jim discovers that happiness is an attitude, and that attitude is controlled by his programs—his choices. Suppose he learns that by consciously making specific choices about his happiness at work, he could feel better about himself, his associates, and his job. Do you think changing his choices about being happy each morning could help?

The answer is not only that it could, but with a little practice, Jim may even be able to give himself the renewed energy and positive mental stamina he needs to *change* his situation—or get a better job. Those choices would throw into motion a physiological mechanism in the brain that would affect Jim both physically and mentally in some very positive ways.

The point here is that happiness is an attitude, and therefore so is unhappiness. And because we affect our attitudes by the choices we make, our own happiness is clearly something we can do something about. If you think you can't, try it. That's the way the brain works.

Happiness is an attitude—*and your attitudes are always up to you!*

Happiness Is Always Up to the Individual

Many people believe that their happiness is a *result* of the circumstances of their lives. Some feel they are "victims" and that their happiness, or unhappiness, is literally in the hands of someone else. Others simply feel that happiness is a reaction to life, rather than a personal choice to create happiness on the inside in spite of what is going on on the outside.

It is true, of course, that what happens to us affects our happiness. Many people live in circumstances in which others around them create negativity or pain. I have a favorite line of Self-Talk that applies directly to this situation: "I replace 'That's life, and there is nothing I can do about it' with the words 'That's my choice, and there is something I can do about it.'"

There is no "they" out there who are plotting to keep our happiness from us. If there is a list entitled *"People Who Deserve To Be Happy,"* everybody's name deserves to be on it.

Happiness is a right of life. It is a right that is given to you the moment you enter this world, and it stays with you throughout each moment of each day. You deserve it, and it is yours. But whether you deserve to *have* it or not will always be up to you.

No one else has the right to determine your happiness for you, to give it to you, or to take it away. Other people can affect your happiness—positively or negatively—if you allow them to or encourage them to. But no one has the right to own your happiness but you; it is yours and yours alone.

That is why it does not work to expect or demand that others give you happiness. They can't. They can add to your life in many wonderful ways and give you reason to create a wealth of happiness within yourself, but it is still your happiness—it is still your choice.

Happiness Is Always a Choice

Your choices about your own happiness will always affect that happiness at two different levels. The first level of happiness is how you feel about yourself right now. It is the kind of happiness that increases when something good happens, and usually goes away when there's a problem.

Some people have a lot of those "moments of happiness"—feeling good at the moment—while others have an abundance of "moments of unhappiness" in any given day. Still others live their lives somewhere in between. They are not often really unhappy, but they don't have many moments of genuine happiness either. When you ask them how life is going, they will usually say, "It's okay," and that's about it.

The other level of happiness that is affected by your own choice is a level of happiness that could be defined as *the pursuit of self-fulfillment.*

This higher level of what we call happiness is that broad and general feeling of well-being that we experience when life is going well for us; we are on track, headed in the right direction, and enjoying the journey along the way. It's a good feeling.

Although this kind of happiness is best found by setting good goals and working to achieve them, it seems almost never to come by accident. It is the result of choosing to live each day of our lives in a worthwhile and self-fulfilling way.

Whether the happiness you are looking for is the moment-to-moment, day-to-day kind or that general overall glow of well-being that puts you at peace with the world, your chance of achieving each of them *improves*— the moment you choose to have them. If you do not choose to have them, you will be left with nothing more than chance itself.

Tomorrow morning, first thing, say to yourself, "I choose to be happy today." And then, now and then during the day, when you think about it, say to yourself, "I choose to be happy right now," and see what happens.

Imagine doing that same thing not only a few times during the day tomorrow, but every day for a week or a month or for a whole year. Do you suppose your life would go a little bit better if you did? I do. If you'd like to have more happiness, go ahead. It's your choice.

"If you have to take time to make a choice, take time.

■

Then make the choice."

24

YOUR PERSONAL BOOK OF CHOICES

IF YOU WERE TO ATTEND a seminar or a class in which you were asked to write out a list of the choices you would really like to make right now, what would they be?

What you write would be interesting and revealing. And it would certainly be worthwhile.

In the following few pages, you have the opportunity to list for yourself some of your choices.

This short list of choices will cover only a few of the many important ones that tell you who you are *now,* what you *really* want now, and what you choose to do about it.

This list is a small first step, but it is an important step. The choices you are asked to make in the following pages are "cornerstone" choices—they define your direction and they set you up to recognize and define the rest of the choices that are yours to make—and then to make them. They are just the beginning.

To make the best use of *Your Personal Book of Choices,* I would suggest that you do one of the following:

1. Write your choices in the pages of this book. Keep in mind, of course, that some of the choices that you write may be very personal—for your

eyes only. If you write your choices in the book, you will be writing part of this book yourself. It will be, and should remain, yours and yours alone, unless you choose to share it with someone else.

2. Make a photocopy of the following pages and write your choices on the copy. If you choose to share the book with family members or friends, the choices you write down will stay in your personal file, available for you to reread and review.

3. In the following section, you may choose *not* to write down your choices. You may not have the time right now (and it *should* take some time). If that is the case, read each of the choices that you are asked to make, consider them carefully, give them some thought, and for now, "write" them in your mind.

If you are, however, serious about recognizing and defining your own choices, set an hour or so aside at a later time, reread this chapter, and take the time to fill in the blanks either in the book or on separate sheets of paper. Writing something down often clarifies thoughts. There is no doubt that the time you take to write down some of the most important choices you will ever make in your life could prove to be some of the most valuable time you will ever spend for yourself and on your future.

Whichever method you decide to use, write your choices in the "now"—in the *present tense*. As an example, instead of writing as one of your choices, "I want to spend more time with my family," say "I choose to spend more time with my family." Or, you may be even more specific and say, "I choose to spend at least three nights a week with my family," or even "I spend three nights a week with my family."

Some of the choices you write are those you may not be acting on yet, but even if you're not, write them in the present tense *as though each choice is something you already do*.

As difficult or as easy as it may be for us to write things, it is the process of writing them down that gets us to focus our thoughts. And it helps us clarify what we really want to say.

Your Personal Book of Choices

The next few pages are entirely yours. Whether you write your choices out—in the book, or on a copy of the pages—or just think about them, these pages—and your choices—are yours alone.

My Personal
Book
of
Choices

■

Name_____

Date_____

PART ONE

MY FAMILY AND PERSONAL RELATIONSHIPS

■

A. Family

Examples:

My family is one of the greatest blessings in my life. I choose to make my family important to me.

I enjoy spending time with my family.

My choices about my family are:

_____

_____

_____

_____

_____

_____

_____

_____

_____

B. Primary Personal Relationship

Examples:

I choose to make my relationship beautiful. I choose to make it work and make it last.

I add something special to my relationship every day.

My choices about my most important personal relationship (mate, spouse, friend, etc.) are:

_____

_____

_____

_____

_____

_____

_____

_____

_____

C. Friends

Examples:

I attract people to me who are honest and sincere.

I value my friendships.

I make friends easily.

My choices about the way I treat and deal with my friends are:

_____

_____

_____

_____

_____

_____

_____

_____

_____

_____

PART TWO
My Work, Job, Career, or Position
■

A. Present Work or Career

Examples:

I choose to like my job—and it shows.

I always work to improve myself and get better at what I do.

My choices about my daily work are:

_____

_____

_____

_____

_____

_____

_____

_____

_____

_____

B. Working at Home

Examples:

I take pride in the work I do at home and enjoy spending time there.

I choose to devote my time to the raising of my children. I place high value on the time and effort I share with them.

My choices about working at home are:

_____

_____

_____

_____

_____

_____

_____

_____

_____

C. Future Work or Career Goals

Examples:

I choose to stay in the field I am in now and prepare myself for a top position in it.

I choose to change my job.

My choices about my future career goals or directions are:

_____

_____

_____

_____

_____

_____

_____

_____

_____

PART THREE

MY HEALTH, FITNESS, AND APPEARANCE

A. Health

Examples:

I choose to be healthy, so I keep myself that way.

I allow myself plenty of rest. I am good at recognizing and controlling stress in my life.

I always take time to relax when I need to.

My choices about my health are:

_____

_____

_____

_____

_____

_____

_____

_____

_____

B. Physical Fitness

Examples:

I choose to enjoy exercising every day.

I choose to keep my body in the best possible condition, and I feel great!

My choices about my physical fitness are:

_____

_____

_____

_____

_____

_____

_____

_____

_____

C. Appearance

Examples:

I look good!

I choose to keep myself in shape and looking sharp.

My choices about my appearance are:

_____

_____

_____

_____

_____

_____

_____

_____

_____

_____

PART FOUR

MY INCOME AND THE WAY I MANAGE MONEY

A. Income

Example:

I deserve to increase my income, and I choose to do something about it.

My choices about my income are:

_____

_____

_____

_____

_____

_____

_____

_____

_____

B. Handling Money

Examples:

I manage money well.

I put at least $_____ each month into savings.

I never spend more than I earn.

My choices about the way I manage money are:

_____

_____

_____

_____

_____

_____

_____

_____

_____

PART FIVE

MY PERSONAL OR SPARE TIME

■

Examples:

I always make sure that I set aside enough spare time for myself.

I enjoy my hobby of _____, and I spend at least 3 hours each week on this hobby.

My choices about my spare time are:

_____

_____

_____

_____

_____

_____

_____

_____

PART SIX

THE KIND OF PERSON I AM

■

Examples:

I choose to be happy.

I am sincere.

I am prompt. I am very capable, and I get a lot done.

My choices about the kind of person I am are:

_____

_____

_____

_____

_____

_____

_____

_____

_____

_____

_____

_____

_____

_____

_____

PART SEVEN
MY EDUCATION, TALENTS, AND SKILLS

A. Education

Examples:

I am happy with my formal education, but I choose to continue to attend classes and seminars that improve my knowledge.

I enjoy learning new things.

My choices about my education are:

_____

_____

_____

_____

_____

_____

_____

_____

_____

_____

B. Talents

Examples:

I have many talents, and I like being good at what I do.

I choose to seek new talents in myself; I believe in my ability to do many things well.

My choices about my talents are:

_____

_____

_____

_____

_____

_____

_____

_____

_____

C. Skills

Examples:

I choose to spend time learning new skills and maintaining those I have already mastered.

I can do anything I try to do. I believe in me!

My choices about my skills are:

_____

_____

_____

_____

_____

_____

_____

_____

_____

_____

_____

PART EIGHT
MY SERVICE TOWARD OTHERS
■

Examples:

I believe I have a responsibility to help others, and I enjoy fulfilling that responsibility as often as possible.

When I help others, I am cheerful and enthusiastic—and I never expect something in return.

My choices about the service and support that I offer to others are:

_____

_____

_____

_____

_____

_____

_____

_____

_____

_____

PART NINE
MY SPIRITUAL LIFE AND MY PERSONAL INSPIRATION

■

Examples:

I read at least one book every month that inspires me to live my life in a better way.

I make sure that I spend time each night in personal devotion.

My choices about the spiritual and inspirational areas in my life are:

_____

_____

_____

_____

_____

_____

_____

_____

_____

_____

PART TEN

THE WAY I LIVE EACH DAY

■

Examples:

I am truly thankful for each new day, so I greet it with a smile!

I choose to live each day in the most worthwhile and beneficial way possible—in everything I do.

My choices for the way I live each day are:

_____

_____

_____

_____

_____

_____

_____

_____

_____

Parts Eleven and Twelve are for your special areas of choice. Fill in your title and complete the page with choices that deal with the special subject area you have selected.

PART ELEVEN

My choices about _____ *are:*

_____

_____

_____

_____

_____

_____

_____

_____

_____

PART TWELVE

My choices about _____ *are:*

_____

_____

_____

_____

_____

_____

_____

_____

_____

In your personal book of choices, the answers you give—the choices you make—are your personal prescription from you, to you, on how you choose—right now—to live your life.

If you were to write out all of your choices, those choices would fill an entire book. If you did that you would not only have written a complete book of your choices, you would have written the story of the life you would most like to live.

Fortunately, none of us has to write that book for printed pages. The choices you make are the story of your life that you write in your mind.

Write your story! And write it for yourself. It was always yours to write in the first place—why not go ahead and write it now? No one else will ever have the right to write your story for you. Your choices, your story, have always been and will always be up to you.

"The end result of your life here on earth will always be the sum total of the choices you made while you were here."

25

THE SECRET OF NACI AND T'NACI— THE FINAL CHOICE

WE BEGAN THIS JOURNEY through the choices we make with the story of Naci and T'naci—two young men who were given, as their greatest gift in life, a small but important list of choices that each of them could use to find success—the fullness of life. One of them found it; the other did not.

What Makes the Difference?

Why did Naci succeed, and why did his twin brother T'naci flounder along the way? They were similar in so many ways. They were given the same chances and the same choices. And yet Naci found a way to rise above the adversities of life and reach a little more of the potential that is in all of us, while T'naci did not.

What was the difference? Why do some of us find the best in ourselves and live it out, day by day, while others do not?

Life is a series of choices that build us up, pull us down, or help us do nothing more than break even. All of life, every moment of it, is choices. What we make of those choices is what we make of ourselves.

The choices you make today and tomorrow and

every day thereafter will, without question, *create the picture of who you are, what you want, and what you will do with the life you have to live*.

That puts a lot of responsibility on each of us. It says, quite simply, that like it or not, your life and what you do with it is up to you. It depends on the choices you make.

The Final Choice

If you were to decide right now, at this very moment, that for the rest of your life you will recognize your choices and make them for yourself, there is a good chance that the rest of your life could prosper in almost immeasurable ways. That can happen. You can trust it. But it will happen for you only if you recognize and understand one small but incredibly important final choice.

This one final choice is not a choice that is new to us. We knew about this choice long ago. Of all the choices we have discussed, this one choice is the most important. It is the choice that says:

I believe that I CAN!

or

I believe that I CAN'T!

In our story, Naci and T'naci were both given the same choices in life. Naci believed that he *could*, and T'naci believed that he could *not*.

Whether each of them could succeed in life or not was always and finally determined by what each of them believed most about himself. *Who they believed they were within themselves controlled and determined each of the choices they made.*

Why did one brother succeed when the other brother did not? (If you have not guessed by now, take the letters of each of their names and reverse their order. Naci's name, when spelled in reverse, reads *"I can."* T'naci's name, when spelled in reverse, reads *I can't."*

■

The final choice that will create the foundation for every other choice you will ever make is the choice that says, "I can" or "I can't."

The success you have in making any choice you ever make will always depend on the choice you make to believe in yourself. It is that one simple choice—*the choice to believe in yourself*—that will always help you find the *strength*, the *determination*, the *reason*, and the *vision* to make your choices and your dreams come true.

You were born with all of the potential you will ever need to make your life an *incredible* life. Why not do it? The rest of your life is most certainly up to you. It is your choice. It is your life.

"If each of us did nothing
more than to take
responsibility for ourselves,
none of us would have to
wish that we could change
the world."

ABOUT THE AUTHOR

SHAD HELMSTETTER, a behavioral researcher, author and lecturer in the field of motivational behavior, created a major breakthrough to "Self-Management" in his best-selling book, *What to Say When You Talk to Yourself*. His bestselling *The Self-Talk Solution* includes more than 2,000 personal Self-Talk phrases that offer powerful direction in areas of personal need or interest. Shad is the Chairman of The Self-Talk Institute, a nonprofit organization that develops Self-Talk programs for schools, businesses and other organizations nationwide. He is a featured guest on radio and television programs throughout the United States and is one of the most requested speakers in the country today. In *Predictive Parenting*, Shad showed parents how to use the power of words to give loving, supportive, practical encouragement to their children and to help them actualize their unlimited potential to become well-adjusted, happy and productive adults. His latest hardcover, *Inner Youth: Finding the Fountain of Youth Inside Yourself*, is a revolutionary program that shows us how to tap into the secrets of truly vital living so that we grow *younger* every day—no matter what our age! It will be available from Pocket Books in October 1990.

For information on CHOICES Seminar Programs or to receive a free Special Information Cassette on Self-Talk, write to The Self-Talk Institute, Dept. C, P.O. Box 5165, Scottsdale, AZ 85261, or call 1-800-624-5846.

BESTSELLING AUTHOR OF
WHAT TO SAY WHEN
YOU TALK TO YOURSELF
SHAD HELMSTETTER

Psychologist Shad Helmstetter is a brilliant motivational speaker, columnist and author who has helped millions to take control of their lives, solve problems, accomplish goals and achieve inner direction and motivation with his bestselling books.

Learn the powerful new technique of Self-Talk—positive self messages with Shad Helmstetter.

- ☐ **FINDING THE FOUNTAIN OF YOUTH INSIDE YOURSELF** ....74620-0/$4.99
- ☐ **THE SELF TALK SOLUTION** ....72757-5/$5.99
- ☐ **WHAT TO SAY WHEN YOU TALK TO YOURSELF** ....70882-1/$5.99
- ☐ **CHOICES** ....67419-6/$5.99
- ☐ **PREDICTIVE PARENTING**...................................67970-8/$8.95

Available in Hardcover

- ☐ **YOU CAN EXCEL IN TIMES OF CHANGE** 70338-2/$17.00

POCKET
B O O K S

Simon & Schuster, Mail Order Dept. BSH
200 Old Tappan Rd., Old Tappan, N.J. 07675

Please send me the books I have checked above. I am enclosing $_____ (please add 75¢ to cover postage and handling for each order. Please add appropriate local sales tax). Send check or money order—no cash or C.O.D.'s please. Allow up to six weeks for delivery. For purchases over $10.00 you may use VISA: card number, expiration date and customer signature must be included.

Name _____

Address _____

City _____ State/Zip _____

VISA Card No. _____ Exp. Date _____

Signature _____ 47-07